Strategic Design
for
Student Achievement

Strategic Design
for
Student Achievement

TOURO COLLEGE LIBRARY
Bay Shore

Michael S. Moody
Jason M. Stricker

Teachers College, Columbia University
New York and London

BS

Published by Teachers College Press, 1234 Amsterdam Avenue, New York, NY 10027

Copyright © 2009 by Teachers College, Columbia University

Library of Congress Cataloging-in-Publication Data

Moody, Michael S.
    Strategic design for student achievement / Michael S. Moody, Jason M.
    Stricker.
        p. cm.
    Includes bibliographical references and index.
    ISBN 978-0-8077-4925-8 (pbk. : alk. paper)
        1. Teacher participation in curriculum planning—United States.
    2. Effective teaching—United States. 3. Academic achievement—United States.
    I. Stricker, Jason M. II. Title.
    LB2806.15.M66 2009
    371.102—dc22   2008032907

ISBN 978-0-8077-4925-8 (paper)

Printed on acid-free paper
Manufactured in the United States of America

16   15   14   13   12   11   10   09   8   7   6   5   4   3   2   1

12/19/11

We dedicate this book to the countless teachers committed
to making a difference in the lives of young people every day.

Contents

Acknowledgments

We would first like to thank our colleagues at Insight Education Group. Specifically, Valerie Braimah and Susan Kwon played an instrumental role in the refinement of our thinking. They continued to support us while pushing us to reexamine and redevelop certain aspects of the Strategic Design process. Perhaps more importantly, their talents as teachers and facilitators are truly inspiring.

The teachers we have worked with over the last several years have provided us with invaluable feedback that has continued to inform our work. Specifically, we would like to thank the teachers at Livermore Valley Charter School, who were really the first school faculty to fully embrace Strategic Design and make it their own. They are doing amazing things with their students, and have developed into an admirable professional learning community—always pushing themselves to continue learning.

The principals, coaches, and teachers working with students in schools every day deserve continued praise for their commitment to providing high-quality classrooms for their students. We feel very fortunate for having the opportunity to observe so many wonderful classroom teachers. Although this book positions us to help teachers refine their instructional design practices, we have learned more from them than we could ever teach. Their dedication to their students is truly inspiring.

We would also like to thank Shantanu DuttaAhmed, our editor, for his invaluable contributions to this project. He inspired us to take this project from a series of articles to a complete book, and his talents were instrumental in this transformation.

Finally, we owe immeasurable debt to our families: Heather, Emma, Lily, and Olivia Stricker, Ben Patterson, Lauren Moody, Nick Moody, and Bill and Geralyn Moody. Not only have they continued to support our work, but they have managed to maintain their support in light of intensive travel schedules and amidst our frequent absences from home.

What Is Strategic Design for Student Achievement?

This book was written for teachers by teachers. It is predicated on the large body of research that suggests that the *teacher* has the greatest impact on student achievement. And since we know this, we have engaged in a pursuit to build an instructional design model that positions teachers to be decisionmakers and highly effective instructional designers. We are writing this book because we believe that the students in our schools deserve to be successful and to have access to high-quality classrooms, no matter where they live, how much money their parents make, or what color their skin is. As teachers, we are in a position to affect this very change. However, change will never occur until we undergo a radical, yet very basic, shift in how we think about and design classroom instruction.

This book assumes that there is no substitute for a teacher's judgment regarding how to best teach students. It empowers teachers to make thoughtful instructional decisions and provides guidance to teachers as they navigate the myriad of standards and the barrage of messages regarding how to best "teach standards." The decisionmaking process we are referring to is called Strategic Design for Student Achievement.

As you read this book, you'll quickly discover that we assume that standards are here to stay. We place no value judgments on standards. What we have learned is that some standards are more descriptive and specific to a grade level and thus more helpful or informative for a teacher when making instructional decisions based on standards. Regardless of the quality of the writing embodied within the standards, it is incumbent upon teachers to ensure that their instruction is aligned to the standards.

STANDARDS AS A CATALYST FOR ACTION

One of the most valuable contributions that standards have made to the field of education has been their ability to engage educators in thinking through the process of making content accessible to *all* students. This awareness, inherent within the concept of standards themselves, enables us to talk about and discuss with our colleagues what we are teaching and why. Thus, far from creating a rote environment, standards actually initiate professional discussions among colleagues, enhancing the teaching process and the profession itself. We firmly believe that the conversations and work that have resulted from the advent of standards has been invaluable to the field. What began as expectations that were put in place—namely, that all students will have access to high-quality content and must perform at specific levels of proficiency—now allows us to engage in dialogue, as professionals, to ensure that we are doing our best to address those expectations in a collegial atmosphere. Standards have served as a catalyst for this dialogue.

This book is designed to be used by those in the field who have the greatest impact on student achievement—the teacher. It explores an instructional design process teachers can utilize to develop rigorous, standards-based instructional units and lessons. This instructional design process (Strategic Design) is comprised of three stages: Stage One: Prioritizing Standards, Stage Two: Aligning Assessments to Standards, and Stage Three: Designing and/or Choosing Effective Instructional Strategies. The book is organized around these three stages and provides detailed descriptions and examples of each stage. Before we begin to describe the Strategic Design process, we feel that it is important to provide the historical context that surrounds standards-based instruction.

STRATEGIC DESIGN
AS A RESPONSE TO THE STANDARDS MOVEMENT

Good instruction is critical to student success, and the evidence to support this assertion is overwhelming. Thus, above all, the standards-based reform movement must address the overwhelming need for high-quality instruction aimed at providing every child with a world-class education. However, these reform efforts and the knowledge we have gained from them thus far are not without their inherent complications and challenges. There are certain truths we must face head-on if we are to make standards-based reform an effective way of improving American education, a reform movement that can be implemented on a sustained level rather than becoming the cure-all for the day. Strategic Design was created by two teachers who felt they could have a greater impact on students by examining what good teaching "looked like" and facilitating conversations about how to operationalize these findings in classrooms. Our own educational careers began in the classroom as teachers. And like most teachers, we met with varying levels of success. One might attribute our challenges in the early years to a lack of support, to insufficient instructional materials, or simply to our inexperience. However, as we moved into different positions and gained more years under our belt, what we both realized was that there was no single "right way" to teach. Unfortunately, there were no silver bullets. Thus, like all teachers, we realized that we must think about how to teach most effectively—and how to figure out the process for creating lessons that engaged our students. As we left the classroom and moved into positions of teacher support, our eyes were opened to the fact that teachers, no matter what grade level or subject they teach, all face the same questions: How does one create a high-quality, standards-based instructional program? How do we take the theory that is ever-present and make it usable at the classroom level? Strategic Design was developed in response to these questions that surfaced in our teaching experience.

Today we continue our teaching practices through our field work, which presents Strategic Design as an instructional design model based on the fundamental premise that we must provide teachers with the tools necessary to make theories "usable." For the last several years we have focused exclusively on developing a model for instructional design that is teacher-friendly, but also incorporates the theories and practices of the best educational researchers.

Our primary goal through Strategic Design is to maximize teacher potential to do amazing things with kids. Therefore, maintaining a teacher's perspective is vital to the success of our work. And to ensure that we did not lose the perspective that drives this process, we went back into the classroom to teach an 11th-grade American Literature class using the Strategic Design process in order to maintain that very teacher's perspective we speak of. We have worked diligently in the development of Strategic Design to draw on our experiences as teachers and to help people think through how to implement Strategic Design within the context and reality of the classroom. When we created Strategic Design, we certainly took into account a universal set of issues that schools deal with (e.g., NCLB, English Language Learners, special education, classroom management considerations, textbook and other resource use and availability). Our teaching, fieldwork, and explorations of instructional design with teachers all over the country led us to a deep understanding of a need for a process-oriented approach to instructional design, rather than one driven by the development of a "final product." Essentially, Strategic Design is about engaging in a collaborative and thoughtful process for designing instruction that honors the experience and knowledge of the teacher while keeping the goal of student achievement at the center of the conversation.

We have spent several years fine-tuning the model with the intention of creating a stable process for examining the foundations of good instruction rather then thinking up quick-fix strategies for engaging students. We firmly believe that a solid approach to defining instruction, such as Strategic Design, provides teachers with the guidance necessary to develop their own curriculum, relying on their own unique experiences and professional judgments to determine which strategies will best serve them in their own classrooms.

Standards-based instruction is a challenge, to say the least. And in order to fully engage in this process, we must first acknowledge that, contrary to the hopes of legislators and educators involved in the advent of No Child Left Behind, *standards have not proven to be the equalizer they were intended to be.*

The introduction of standards into the field of education, although by no means a new concept, has become the foundation of instructional programs across the country. Standards have become a way of life for educators, particularly in light of recent accountability measures and given the dire need for immediate and large-scale increases in student achievement. The entire spectrum of the standards-based reform efforts, and the impetus behind such efforts, might suggest that standards (and the accountability measures that generally accompany them) would be the panacea to rectify most of the defects in our educational system. Of particular concern are the many problems inherent to an inconsistent curriculum, as well as relying on standards in and of themselves to close the notorious achievement gap. Attending to such optimistic projections is one of the most fundamental assumptions surrounding the use of standards, namely, that through these established standards all students will be receiving the same content, which will enable greater equity among students in the same grade throughout the country. In fact, many believed that standards would prove to be the primary means of closing the achievement gap. The assumption was that many students were not achieving at the same rate as their counterparts because they were not given access to the same "content."

This assumption was not entirely false. We have worked with many teachers at different grade levels whose classroom instruction was comprised solely of the content they were most comfortable with. In fact, as a novice classroom teacher prior to the advent of standards, Michael selected the topics for his middle school science class that he felt would be most interesting to his students. (In actuality, the topics were most interesting to him.) He was not placing the emphasis on what his students would need to know to be successful in their next science class, and he received no guidance in regard to the content he should be teaching. And to further confound the matter, the science teacher next door taught her students about things that she was most interested in—which did not align with Michael's curriculum or that of the high school. We suspect that this scenario was being replicated in almost every school across the country: Students were not being provided access to the same content.

Correspondingly, Michael is quite confident that the high school teachers were asking themselves why his middle school students were not prepared for high school science. Needless to say, we were all intelligent, well-intentioned teachers of middle school science, but we worked in complete isolation, with little if any idea of the big picture. After all, how could we be expected to prepare our middle school students for high school science? The high school teachers were also working in isolation, functioning on the basis of each teacher's individual preferences and prejudices. No one ever alerted Michael to the fact that his students were not receiving critical foundational knowledge. In fact, his teaching reviews were excellent, and he continued to operate the same way, premised on the old saying, "If it ain't broke, don't fix it." In his eyes, his curriculum was working. After all, his classroom continued to function effectively, and on the surface there was nothing to fix. His students appeared to be learning, and he was able to assess their knowledge in terms of what he was teaching and thus determined that for the most part, students were "learning science" in his class. However, as is now clear in retrospect, his students were not necessarily learning the content that would most benefit them as they moved out of his class and into another. In addition, and more importantly, they may not have been learning the content they would be tested on in the standardized exams. Thus, although his students were learning, there were very few means to find out if his students were learning "the right stuff." It would be fair to say, using a pedagogical shorthand, that standards now constitute the "right stuff." Thus, the advent of standards has placed a spotlight on the perhaps obvious but never consciously admitted fact that teachers often teach what they know best, not because they are opposed to teaching anything else, but simply because no one has told them exactly what they need to teach. Is it really any surprise that students arrived on our doorsteps with various levels of prior knowledge, varying levels of interest, and different educational experiences?

The implementation of content standards was premised on the belief that by providing teachers with a common set of learning objectives, we were ensuring that all students, even those in underperforming urban schools, would learn the same things, and thus perform at comparable levels. It is true that standards have provided a guide for teachers with regard to content. However, standards in and of themselves cannot, and will never, be able to ensure student achievement for all students.

Classroom instruction still remains the most direct, and most effective, way to impact student achievement. It did not take long for the education community to realize that standards alone could not serve as the sole means of closing the achievement gap. In fact, our own research and fieldwork in schools across the country has clearly suggested that if schools were not sensitive to these issues, *the conversations related to standards highlighted and widened the gap they were intended to decrease.* The biggest complaint about standards is that students who enter a classroom lacking essential skills, in math for example, will never be able to master grade-level standards. After all, how can students be expected to master Algebra I content standards if they cannot multiply and divide proficiently? As you can see, a simple question can derail the concept that standards alone can equalize education. Many educators automatically dismissed standards as inappropriate or unrealistic, and returned to the practice of teaching what they felt their students needed to learn.

Given these impediments to a post-standard environment, in our opinion it is fair to say that thus far, students have not received equitable opportunities to learn. And while the introduction of standards assists teachers in identifying what their students *should* know and be able to do, standards do not help a given teacher figure out *how* to help students learn everything they should have known prior to entering her classroom in order to ensure that they master the current grade-level content and are deemed proficient learners. The bottom line is that many teachers have been frustrated by standards because they do not provide assistance in assuring that students are provided with equitable learning opportunities. (Something written on a piece of paper does not ensure equitable learning.) In fact, in many instances, standards simply become the barometer of what students don't know and cannot do.

Thus, it is fair to say that standards have not yet proven to be the equalizer they were intended to be. Some might even argue that standards engender inequalities in that they do not account for the fact that many students lack the foundational skills necessary to achieve standard mastery. As educators, this is a disheartening statement and one that is not easy to accept. If standards will not help close the achievement gap, then what will? The question becomes more urgent when, after a consideration of the present state of affairs in education, it does not appear that standards will come and go as many other reform efforts of the past have.

The discontent and failure of standards to equalize education is even more apparent in our work with schools that have been identified as underperforming. During a training in an urban middle school, a discussion developed among the teachers about how "unfair" standards were, especially for the group of minority students they were working with. They felt that these students were at a particular disadvantage because their home life was not one that "valued" education and they lacked the prior knowledge that was necessary to be successful in middle school. The discussion also brought to light the eternal argument that underperformance is the fault of the student's previous school. Without fail, when working with high school teachers we hear, "If only the middle school teachers had prepared these students for high school. Now I have to teach both middle school and high school standards." When working with middle school teachers, we hear the same complaints about elementary school, and the elementary school teachers frame the complaint yet again as, "If only the parents would read to their children. Now we have to teach students the skills they should have picked up before they started school." Of course the complaints come full circle: When working with parents, we hear "If only those teachers would do their job, my child would be able to read and do math at grade level."

These anecdotal voices are yet another example of the fact that in contemporary education, the lack of student achievement is often reduced to a blame game. And quite frankly, the above assertions are not without their own truths. However, what we as educators fail to acknowledge is that perhaps those teachers we blame for underperformance are actually doing the best job they can considering their experience, resources, and training. And before the advent of standards, it was not so much that teachers were ineffective. In fact, they may have been extremely effective but simply teaching content that was not contiguous for the next grade or course. Can we really expect students to have some prior knowledge about photosynthesis if their previous teacher did an amazing job teaching them about dinosaurs? Are we asking for too much? What if, rather than waiting for the decisionmakers to find the silver bullet, we, as teachers, reformed our own classroom practices? What if, quite simply, we stop being frustrated with public education's lack of progress and reform the way we teach? Is it possible that standards can work for us, as individuals and professionals, regardless of whether or not they reform the whole of public education?

In our fieldwork, we have seen teachers transform student achievement using standards-based instruction. We have watched teachers reform their classroom practice by placing standards at the center of their work and then thoughtfully examining what the standards are requiring of them as teachers, in addition to what they require of students. Perhaps if we looked at standards as a means for teachers to examine their practice rather than as a checklist of what students need to know, we would make greater gains. Standards must play a central role in the process of curriculum development. And equally important is the process that teachers must go through of examining content standards, developing assessments, and aligning innovative instruction to those standards. Rather than viewing standards as the great equalizer, we must broaden our view and understand that high-quality instructional design, within the context of standards, is what will transform public education as we know it. Fullan has observed that the "reculturing" of the education system

> involves building new conceptions about instruction (e.g., teaching for understanding and using new forms of assessment) and new forms of professionalism for teachers (e.g., building commitment to continuous learning and to problem-solving through collaboration). (Fullan, 1996, p. 7)

Effective instructional design and implementation founded upon content standards will prove to be the great equalizer that standards alone have not achieved.

Teaching is both an art and a science. And until we begin to understand how these two approaches fit together, the artists and the scientists will continue to struggle to find common ground. We would argue that state content standards are the science, and the teacher's delivery of those standards is the art. One must embrace both in order to be successful in a standards-based system. More importantly, in order for standards to serve as the great equalizer in education, teachers must first be supported in the practice of understanding and using standards in meaningful and creative ways. As we have seen, the standards-based movement brings with it many inherent challenges that schools and districts must overcome. Each of these challenges requires specific attention to developing strategies that will overcome the obstacles that might undermine implementation efforts. It is not, however, an impossible feat. Given our era of standards-based, high-stakes accountability measures, it is critical that educators work diligently to overcome these challenges and rise to the challenge of educating all students in the nation's public schools.

To this point we have talked a great deal about standards and their impact on teachers and teaching. We now want to step back and briefly contextualize standards within the larger context of accountability.

THE ERA OF ACCOUNTABILITY

Not surprisingly, the introduction of standards brought with them an era of increased accountability to ensure that students were performing at the level required by those standards. Indeed, it would be fair to say that standards and accountability function as different aspects of the same process, and one does not take precedence over the other. The discussion of content standards has persisted and taken many forms in American educational history, and issues of accountability have persisted in education for many years as well. However, because of the public and political measures, the era of accountability we have currently entered appears to be without precedence, and the most rigorous the field has ever seen. The introduction of No Child Left Behind, coupled with state-specific accountability measures, has placed a burden on schools like never before. And the individuals who appear to be feeling the most pressure from current accountability measures are, once again, classroom teachers.

Classroom teachers have always known that they are the individuals closest to, and most responsible for, student achievement. Correspondingly, teachers have also been the ones most directly concerned with student achievement: Not a day goes by that teachers do not think about how their students are doing, which students are struggling, and how best to address the specific needs of each of their students. Historically, as teachers, we have simply continued to do our jobs and let the politicians play with accountability and its supposed ramifications as they saw fit. In short, politics and the classroom have been viewed by most teachers as discrete social arenas. While politicians and high-level district administrators toiled with various accountability measures and systems over the years, individual classroom teachers, for the most part, have simply kept on teaching, with little involvement in the political arena. In fact, teachers had hitherto maintained a confidence that the politics of education would never be organized enough to infringe on their individual classroom practices. This "unaccountable" existence for teachers, however, has ended. For the first time, the field of education is universally feeling the effects of accountability. For the first time, what is going on in individual classrooms is being watched, evaluated, and expected to change. Individual teachers are being held accountable for the progress their students are, or are not, making. So it is not surprising that the question that haunts these scrutinized classrooms is more often than not: "Is this really fair?" What about students who come to our classes without basic reading skills? How can we really make up for several years of ineffective instruction?

In the midst of these teacher concerns, the policymakers refrain from providing specific answers and continue to systemically reiterate the need for improvement. Schools that are not performing at minimum levels of proficiency are being closely monitored, and sanctions are being applied with greater force. These schools are expected to produce gains in student achievement, usually within 3 years, or they face a number of significant ramifications. "Program improvement" has become a common occurrence for many schools. And the leaders of these schools must then figure out how to motivate and educate teachers to do a "better" job of educating their students. In our own work, as we have monitored the present situation and thought about increasing student achievement on a large scale, it has become glaringly apparent that teachers need support in order to enact change. Teachers are not deliberately undermining the education of their students. They are simply undersupported and often ill-equipped to put a curriculum program in place that can satisfactorily increase student achievement for all of their students. In turn, this has opened up a huge market for companies to sell their "No Child Left Behind Compliant" wares to schools and districts alike.

Only a few years ago, accountability looked very different than it does today. There was a time when accountability meant the purchase of additional curricular materials or computer programs. For example, a large urban district we worked with adopted a scripted language arts program for grades K–3. At that time, a great deal of money was designated to support the implementation efforts of this program. All of the materials were purchased, including supplemental instructional aids, all of the district teachers were trained, and each school received funding for a full-time reading coach. Millions of dollars were spent in the first 6 months of this adoption. The reading coach became the first "real" symbol of accountability. It was the sole responsibility of the reading coach to ensure that the program was implemented in every classroom with complete fidelity. The coaches were highly trained in the program and spent their days observing the practice of their colleagues. However, there were a few critical flaws with this approach.

To begin with, although the coaches were extensively trained in the program, most had never actually used the program with students. It was a fairly new curriculum program and these coaches were no longer classroom teachers. This immediately threatened their credibility with the teachers they were "supporting" because there was an underlying feeling that they really did not understand how hard it was to teach with the adopted program. The second, and perhaps more devastating, issue was that the coaches were expected to ensure complete fidelity to the program. Unfortunately, fidelity was defined through very concrete (and arguably limiting) indicators. For example, every classroom had the exact same physical layout; every bulletin board was in the same place; letter cards were on the same wall in every classroom. Even more challenging for classroom teachers was the expectation that all teachers would be on exactly the same lesson, on the same day, at the same time. Those who could not comply received written notification of their lapse in effective implementation. It did not take long before the coaches became known as the "reading police." Needless to say, the coaches were viewed as evaluators, not as people who provided support in the mutual effort of better educating students. This view had a necessarily negative and significant impact on the implementation process. Most importantly, this dynamic between the teachers and the coaches negatively impacted teacher support for the program. For 2 years, teachers could not take field trips and all school activities revolved around the sacred English/Language Arts time. The morale of the schools and teachers sank. And in a matter of months teachers were demoralized, frustrated, and resentful.

This is only one example of a district's attempt to raise student achievement through a curriculum adoption and implementation of increased accountability measures. In this particular instance, it is also important to note that, although there was a spike in test scores, the achievement gap remained constant. Eventually, after 2 years, the progress students had been making ultimately leveled off. Again, although this was a well-intentioned attempt at increasing student achievement, the final results lacked any real impact and the increased accountability measures were not enabling in any specific ways.

Similarly, district attempts at accountability, although well intentioned, appear to consistently miss the most important point—that improving teaching practice is a critical component in increasing student achievement. And while districts do acknowledge that teaching practices must change, their means for changing such practices most often come in the form of a new program or product. Rarely do districts or schools dedicate the necessary resources to improving teaching practice through ongoing training and constant support. The bottom line is that it costs too much and takes too much time.

How many years it will take for the field of education to realize that the amount of time and money that has been spent since standards were introduced might have been more productively and thoughtfully spent on ensuring high-quality teaching practice? Teachers, when given the right tools, can hold themselves accountable for results. So far, the invention of standards-aligned textbooks, computer software, comprehensive school reform models, and instructional materials has claimed to be the surefire way to ensure that students are meeting state-mandated expectations. Instructional materials, however, can only do so much. It is the skill of the teacher using the materials that matters most. This type of thinking will require a substantial shift in the current paradigm.

For years research has suggested that teachers have the most significant impact on student achievement. So why has it taken so long to realize that what teachers do in their classrooms is the critical arena that must be analyzed and further enabled? We believe that the short answer is that while the classroom is the most critical element in education, it is also the most dynamic, and thus, on some levels, the most difficult to assess precisely and determine what must be improved. Perhaps it is exactly this unease, created by a lack of quantifiable data on *teaching as a practice*, that makes some educators believe it is much easier to create a standards-aligned textbook than to help teachers really examine their teaching practices and make the necessary changes to increase the achievement of their students. Even as we write this, it is an overwhelming statement to consider.

However, we must learn to think within larger and more comprehensive frames about how to help our students learn. If we stop thinking pragmatically for just a second, perhaps we will realize that pragmatism has never closed the achievement gap, and it never will. We must dream of ways to enact true change, and then think pragmatically about how to operationalize that dream. Our dream is to transform teaching practice in such a way that teachers are effective designers of their own curriculum. Our dream is one in which schools provide the resources and time necessary for teachers to craft instructional opportunities for students in which they master standards within a rich learning community. Our dream is to find a process for enabling teachers to become masterful in their craft without stripping away their dignity, experience, or creativity. Strategic Design is the realization of this dream.

DESCRIPTION OF THE BOOK

The ensuing chapters present the Strategic Design process from beginning to end.

Chapter 1 presents the historical catalysts in the field of education that have led to the development of the Strategic Design process, and the question that has primacy in that process, namely: "How can teachers retain creative control over their instructional design in the era of standards and accountability?" As an answer to this question, the chapter frames teachers as curriculum designers, as opposed to mere deliverers of prescriptive programs. This is followed by an overview of the process itself and its objectives; the three stages that inscribe the process: analyzing and prioritizing content standards, aligning assessments to standards, and designing rigorous and engaging instruction; and the critical importance of Benjamin Bloom's taxonomy to the levels of cognition and his integral structural importance to Strategic Design. We end Chapter 1 with a discussion of those scholars in the field whose work has been most influential on our own thinking as we developed Strategic Design.

Chapter 2 initiates Stage One of the Strategic Design process. We begin by describing the benefits of prioritizing standards and explain what we mean by the process. In this chapter the work of prioritizing standards is broken down into five discrete steps that take the reader through the process of prioritizing in explicit ways. The five critical steps of the prioritization process include: careful reading of the standards, a critical understanding of content, application of Bloom's taxonomy, aligning the levels of cognition in Bloom's to the standards, and finally asking a series of key questions that refine the prioritization process even further. Chapter 2 concludes by describing the clustering process (which follows prioritization), and explaining how standards are clustered both within the same grade level/content area and across grade levels/content areas.

Chapter 3 is concerned with various aspects of assessing student achievement, and represents Stage Two of the Strategic Design process. This chapter describes fully a critical aspect of this instructional design process, namely that within our model the designing of assessment takes place prior to instruction. We explain the value and efficacy of initiating this temporal shift in the instructional design process. Chapter 3 also explains the importance of selecting appropriate assessments to measure student mastery, as well as providing the methods that ensure that the assessments we choose are indeed measuring what we intend and need. This section is followed by an in-depth discussion of the four types of available assessments—selected response assessment, constructed response assessment, performance assessment, and personal communication—detailing the advantages and disadvantages of each. Chapter 3 concludes by describing the process of aligning assessment to standards.

Chapter 4 is the third and final stage of Strategic Design. This chapter presents the philosophical premise behind our concept of instruction, a premise that (re)configures the teacher as one who is a facilitator of instruction, as opposed to one who delivers information or is primarily a lecturer. We first present a discussion of utilizing formative assessments as the first step in understanding and identifying appropriate instructional strategies. We also present our model for creating SMART objectives for instruction, the acronym representing five critical aspects of defining useful and standards-aligned learning objectives: Specific, Measurable, Aligned to standards, Realistic, and Time-bound. Chapter 4 concludes by presenting three key questions as a way of ensuring that the instructional activities chosen are indeed productive to our aims.

Chapter 5 presents our own analysis of the process of Strategic Design as we reflect on our own experiences, both as scholars and as practitioners in the field. Indeed, this chapter has a critical section on the importance of the practice of reflection itself. We hope that our answers provide a cogent narrative of who we are and what motivates us to work in the field of education, as well as the ways in which we see the continuing evolution of the Strategic Design process. Chapter 5 also presents, in an encapsulated form, one of our success stories: the utilization of the process at Livermore Valley Charter School.

Chapter 6 summarizes the key elements of Strategic Design and reinforces the concept that this process is about creating the type of high-quality classroom instruction that all students deserve. This chapter describes how Strategic Design has been informed by the best thinking in the field—including the many classroom teachers we have worked with—and was designed in response to the pervasive dilemma of attempting to implement too many "research-based" instructional programs simultaneously. In addition, this chapter provides the reader with an understanding of how teachers have responded to this instructional design process. Finally, we foreshadow potential future scholarship related to Strategic Design, such as the implementation of school structures that can accommodate and support the implementation of the process.

CHAPTER 1

How Will Strategic Design Benefit My Teaching Practice?

Ms. Kwon, an experienced and much-loved science teacher, was teaching her favorite unit on the digestive system. She had planned several engaging activities for her students during the 3-week unit, culminating with the much-anticipated dissection of a frog. Students would wait all year for this unit, and Ms. Kwon was known for her dramatic buildup to the big event.

On the big day, not a single student was absent. Students sat quietly at their desks while Ms. Kwon explained the lab. Eagerly, students commenced with the dissection. According to Ms. Kwon's rubric, success in this project would be indicated by having students identify and label the various parts of the digestive system. When the class period was over, Ms. Kwon was very proud of the fact that her students, even some of those currently failing her course, had successfully completed the project according to her expectations. More notably, she was proud of the fact that almost every single student had been engaged from the opening of class through the final bell.

The dissection project was inevitably followed by the district's benchmark assessment examinations. When the district test scores for Ms. Kwon's students arrived on her desk, she was dismayed by the fact that her students had not performed as well as she had expected. In fact, the assessment results revealed that nearly 60% of her students had not demonstrated mastery of the state standards related to the digestive system. Ms. Kwon could not help but feel that this was yet another example of how standardized tests endemically fail to accurately measure student knowledge. After all, her students had been totally engaged with the unit on the digestive system, and they had done well on her own assessment rubrics. Thus, she concluded, they must have learned the content.

In response to the disappointing test results, Ms. Kwon's principal asked her to review a new curriculum program that was aligned to the state science standards. While the principal recognized the power of Ms. Kwon's classroom activities and her unfailing ability to engage her students, the principal remained understandably concerned about all students meeting the established standards. Thus, wary of intruding on what appeared to be a successful classroom, she reluctantly advised Ms. Kwon that a more structured science curriculum might help her students be more successful on the district tests. Ms. Kwon was frustrated and concerned by the fact that state and district accountability could now potentially interfere with her ability to use those creative and engaging instructional approaches and methods that had been the hallmark of her teaching.

How can teachers like Ms. Kwon retain creative control over their instructional design while ensuring that students attain mastery of content standards?

TEACHERS AS CURRICULUM DESIGNERS

The tension between teacher control and standards-based curriculum has existed for years as educational reformers have sought strategies that balance teacher design with the consistency and continuity offered by prepackaged, standards-based curricular materials. Indeed, it is hard to imagine a contemporary field of study more fraught with reform movements than education. With the introduction of numerous mandated accountability methods, schools are constantly challenged to improve student achievement. Funding, scarcity of time-tested resources and methodologies, and a lack of "highly qualified" teachers are only a few of the obstacles to implementing curricular programs that successfully increase student achievement. As educators, we have found ourselves constantly frustrated with the revolving door of programs aimed at meeting the needs of our students. We have become tired of working to implement the latest and greatest program, only to find out that yet another, newer program has been mandated and we will be expected to implement it in only a few months.

Since the introduction of accountability measures, many teachers have felt as if they are being stripped of individuality, creativity, and professional freedom. Teachers have struggled to maintain creative control over classroom instruction in the midst of potential intrusions into the pedagogical process. And as soon as district officials realized that the introduction of content standards alone could not single-handedly increase student achievement, they began identifying ways to close the ever-widening achievement gap. What was unfortunate about most of these attempted solutions was that very few of them attempted to materially involve the expertise of the classroom teacher.

Often, publishers specializing in education attempted to fill the gap by providing any number of curriculum programs whose alignment to standards was supposedly the panacea for what ailed our classrooms. States began adopting specific curricular programs and textbooks that required less design by teachers. In fact, many of them provided scripts for teachers to follow. The idea of following a script was perceived as both a blessing and a curse.

For many new teachers, and even veteran teachers uncomfortable with standards-based reform movements, the script initially provided an element of comfort. The introduction of scripted programs allowed teachers to adjust to standards-based instruction without having to take immediate and complete control over what was being taught within a standards-aligned context. Essentially, and most noticeably at the elementary level, professional development for teachers shifted away from curriculum design to training on how best to follow a prepublished program. Both the emotional and material impact of such a shift is best exemplified by the words of one 4th-grade teacher who told us, "My college acting class was more helpful during my first year of teaching than my entire credentialing program."

This shift from instructor-generated curriculum design to prepackaged programs also complicated the accountability picture in unforeseen ways, because when educators realized that students were not succeeding, they had the publishers of these programs to blame. And in turn, the publishers asserted that the lack of progress was due to ineffective implementation at the site level, and not a deficiency in the programs they had produced. Once again, the field of education was mired in a blame game, with everyone having someone to defer responsibility to.

The bottom line was that the various accountability scenarios did very little, if anything, to improve classroom instruction. The only discernible effect of the various accountability movements was the frequent adoption of the newest program being promoted as the latest panacea for increasing student achievement. As a result, teachers were frustrated yet again with the fact that as soon as they had mastered a specific program, yet another new program was purchased, and consequently, additional teacher training ensued.

In short, if you take teaching out of the hands of teachers and delegate the process to a series of scripted and mandatory instructions, how can teachers be blamed for the lack of student success? The fact that teachers could no longer be held responsible for the lack of student improvement relieved some and frustrated others. But the most pernicious message from these confusing and sporadic attempts to raise student achievement was that teachers felt that they were no longer to be professionally trusted to teach. Shifting to prepackaged teaching programs seemed to suggest that the potential success of students had become the responsibility of textbook publishers and not the teachers themselves. As we stated above, while such a dynamic might at times appear to be a relief to a profession that seemed almost perpetually under siege, the general distrust that this state of affairs implied with regard to the teaching profession was ultimately humiliating. It has been our overwhelming experience that teachers take their jobs very seriously and strive to act in the best interest of students. For the most part, teachers are open to new ideas and understand that even the mandatory programs are symptomatic of the atmosphere of accountability that they must necessarily function within. However, without the appropriate guidance, support, and resources, instructional design becomes at best inconsistent and sporadic, and at worst ineffective.

Undeniably, the shift to prescriptive classroom resources strips both responsibility as well as creativity from teachers. This sense of a lack of control and the right to assert one's professional discretion in the classroom is one of the most common complaints voiced by educators in this era of standards and accountability. No doubt some could reasonably argue, and indeed they have, that if standards-based reform efforts are helping the students, then we need not heed teacher complaints. The trajectory of such debates is mitigated by the all-too-familiar "the ends justify the means" approach. However, what proponents of such arguments dismiss is that to date there is very little empirical evidence to suggest that any of the current reform efforts have significantly and verifiably increased student achievement. Definitely, there have been instances of success, but the field as a whole is still faced with the challenge of improving public education to the level that it can provide equal opportunities for all students to succeed. Over time, what we have come to realize is that while specific curricular programs have played a role in raising student achievement, we have yet to accomplish what is most consequential: ensuring that all students are achieving at equal levels. It would seem that finally the profession is acknowledging what it has always known—the teacher, not the textbook, is one of the most significant factors in promoting classroom learning and increasing student achievement. As we have been discussing, the trend in curriculum reform, to move away from teacher-driven design toward increasingly prescriptive curricula and programs, would seem to abandon the basic truth about the primacy of teachers in the classroom. In a report on "The Real Value of Teachers," the Education Trust cites a 1996 study by W. L. Sanders and J. C. Rivers that states that:

> So large was the impact of teachers on student learning that it exceeded any one thing about the students themselves . . . teacher effectiveness is "the single biggest factor influencing gains in achievement," an influence bigger than race, poverty, parent's education, or any of the other factors that are often thought to doom children to failure. (Carey, 2004, p. 4)

Having made a case for the critical importance of the teacher in raising student achievement, we have developed a process that puts the power of instruction back in the hands of teachers. It is our belief that we must abandon the total reliance we have developed on scripted programs, so-called "standards-aligned" textbooks, or computer-based intervention programs to teach our students. While these resources have their value, they are just that—resources, not miraculous panaceas for all that ails the pedagogical process. We must remember that these programs and the variety of available aids are additional supports to an already high-quality curriculum, but that these sources of support cannot be a viable substitute for an effective curriculum. It is important to shift our energies toward what is most important—training teachers to utilize their individual knowledge, experience, and creativity to strategically design standards-based classroom instruction.

Based on the high-quality work of researchers in the field and the work of inspirational and dedicated teachers, we have developed Strategic Design for Student Achievement (Strategic Design). This process-oriented model makes the latest research on quality instructional practices available to classroom teachers. We are not attempting to reinvent the wheel. Rather, we are extending the thinking of our colleagues to present a model of instructional design that is user-friendly and both adaptable and applicable to the needs of individual teachers and their classrooms.

STRATEGIC DESIGN AS A WAY OF THINKING

To put it quite simply, Strategic Design is a way of thinking. The Strategic Design process is the art and science of teaching, finally combined as teaching praxis. It is not a program or a product. It is not a foolproof plan or a silver bullet for increasing student achievement. It is not easy. It requires extensive thinking and hard work. It is a three-stage process for engaging teachers in the important work of critically examining state content standards (Stage One), aligning classroom assessment systems to ensure that we are assessing for mastery (Stage Two), and designing lessons that provide the necessary skills and knowledge for students to be successful (Stage Three). We say it is a way of thinking because our work with teachers has shown us that we must often let go of the comfortable routines of designing instruction and rethink how we teach. This is hard work for most. But it is the necessary work that must be done in order to meet the needs of our students and the expectations of the existing accountability systems our communities have enacted.

Strategic Design is a comprehensive way of thinking about standards, communicating with our colleagues, directing student learning, and delivering classroom instruction. The value of the process lies in its ability to bring out the best in teachers and transform that thinking into high-quality, standards-based units of instruction. We are not asking you to drop everything and try our "new program." We are simply challenging you to use this book as a means of examining your current practice and becoming an even more effective educator than you already are.

With almost every group we work with, teachers express resistance as we introduce the process. Teachers are already teaching—therefore, why do they need someone else to come into their school and change things up again? And at this point in time, all teachers are "teaching standards." However, it does not take long for educators to realize that this process is not about throwing away our teaching experience and starting from scratch. In fact, successful application of the Strategic Design process is reliant on a teacher's experience and professional judgment. This is a process, not a program, and it is designed to meet teachers where they are. It utilizes the best thinking and teaching of everyone on the team. The Strategic Design process provides a structure for rethinking how we have approached standards, examining how we will ensure full implementation of standards, and determining how our current teaching practices can be utilized or modified within this new model. This process places a high premium on the fact that all teachers come to the table as professionals, and the process treats them as professionals. It values their knowledge, experience, and willingness to look critically within their current teaching practice in order to fine-tune it so as to ensure that it is standards-based and truly innovative.

STRATEGIC DESIGN TO
PRESERVE INDIVIDUALITY AND CREATIVITY

Strategic Design takes teachers beyond what they're used to. Almost every teacher we have worked with has commented about how the process really challenged their practice in a positive way. We don't think this is rocket science—or the only way to design instruction. There are hundreds of models for designing classroom instruction. We are, however, very proud of the fact that this model allows teachers to maintain their individual voice and creativity throughout the process while empowering them to meet the demands of increased accountability and state mandates. Our model views state mandates as a challenge to improve "our game."

Every teacher brings a wealth of knowledge and experience to the table. Strategic Design is not the next "best" curriculum program. It is merely a process for engaging teachers in work and allowing them to spend time learning from one another and the process. Strategic Design for Student Achievement empowers teachers to be the designers of curriculum, not mere recipients of someone else's work. We firmly believe that teacher involvement in the development process is the critical factor that is most often overlooked. Teachers must be given the training, time, and resources to develop their own curriculum and make informed decisions about which resources will most effectively assist them in enabling students to access the content to the point of mastery.

Today, we are at a point where we must realize that along with creative control comes responsibility. This is clearly a case of "be careful what you ask for." However, we must now step up to the challenge to retain the right to design our own curriculum and teach in a manner that best suits our style and personality. From what we have witnessed in our work with teachers, it is our belief that the process of Strategic Design ensures that we can hold onto this privilege.

THE APPLICATION AND PROCESS OF STRATEGIC DESIGN

Strategic Design involves teachers in the dissection and analysis of the standards in order to clarify and identify the multiple concepts that are often embedded within a given standard. By pulling apart the standards and looking at them in relation to Bloom's taxonomy, we can begin to make explicit what the standard is asking students to understand and master. So often, teachers will tell us that they are confident that their instructional design is operating within the relevant parameters of a standards-based classroom because they have read through the list of standards to be sure that they have accounted for the skills students must know at the end of the unit, lesson, or grade level. In essence, the standards are treated as a checklist that the teacher consults to ensure that she or he is covering everything on that standards-based list.

However, after acquiring a working understanding of the deeper way standards are initially approached and conceptualized within the Strategic Design process, these same teachers realize that their lessons are not clearly and directly related (sometimes not at all related) to what the standards are really demanding of them and their students. In mentioning this, by no means are we implying that teachers are lazy, uninterested, or not intelligent enough to ensure that their students master the standards. In fact, what we are suggesting is that the process of Strategic Design provides teachers with the tools to enhance them professionally and enables them to systematically analyze the standards. No one has ever taught us what to do with standards—we have just been told that we need to use them to guide our pedagogical practices. And no doubt, given the insistence on accountability, some teachers view standards as an impediment to their professional duties, rather than something intended to productively guide them in their instructional practices. As we stated, the Strategic Design process provides the tools to thoroughly analyze standards and utilize that analysis toward better instructional design. In so doing, perhaps some aspects of the process also eliminate the hostility with which some in the teaching profession have come to approach standards.

Keeping this in mind, it is critical that teachers are able to engage in a process that allows them to explore and discuss the standards in order to understand exactly what they are demanding. This is not an unfamiliar undertaking for teachers, since the process is very much like teaching itself. In our classroom, it would never be a part of our teaching strategy to hand our students a math book and tell them, "In life, use the math skills in this book." Although the example may initially seem absurd, it is not far off from the way in which many in the field are presently approaching teachers. It is as if we are handing teachers a list of standards with the directive: "In your professional life, you must use these." Given the variety of pressures that teachers are under, be it having to produce accountable results or weathering the most recent political firestorm, we forget that the concept of "standards" (and the ensuing list of standards) is relatively new. If teachers are to thoroughly understand standards, and learn how to effectively utilize them in their teaching, they must be provided with the time and the appropriate training. The various stages and processes endemic to Strategic Design provide that training.

As professionals, it is important for teachers to remember that while standards prescribe what should be taught, they do not inherently prescribe the methods or materials that are to be used to teach the content and skills contained within the standard. Because of the proliferation of the ready-made and prepackaged "teaching aids" that are now available, the confusion in the profession between what to teach and how to teach should not come as a surprise. Our approach with Strategic Design is reliant on understanding the critical distinction between the "what" and the "how." Instead of providing a prescriptive plan, the processes within Strategic Design are premised on the belief that when teachers carefully examine and understand standards, they can effectively align their curriculum to those standards. This opens the door to endless possibilities in terms of the ways in which teachers can address standards through their instructional practices in their classrooms. While there are many positive ways in which Strategic Design impacts teaching practice, we have classified the benefits into the following three broad statements:

- Strategic Design reframes the conversation about standards to one that is constructive rather than compliant.

- Strategic Design provides concrete tools teachers can use to clarify what standards are and what they require students to know and be able to do at different grade levels and in different subjects.
- Strategic Design helps teachers understand how to use curricular resources in an effective, nimble manner.

Below is a further discussion of these benefits.

BENEFITS OF USING STRATEGIC DESIGN

Strategic Design reframes the conversation about standards to one that is constructive rather than compliant. As we have discussed, Strategic Design is first and foremost a tool to address and navigate the complex arena of standards in a way that yields productive and results-oriented classrooms. Consequently, teachers who work with Strategic Design feel most positive about the opportunity to interact with standards on a practical level. Through the Strategic Design process, teachers are able to understand standards in a practical way, and the process takes away the sense of threat that standards can sometimes represent. The level of comprehension about standards that can be achieved through Strategic Design is possible because the process provides an opportunity for teachers to understand what the standards are really asking of students, and how teachers as professionals can deliver the instruction that reflects that.

It is the goal of Strategic Design to provide a concrete sense of direction on how to use the standards and eliminate feelings of being constrained by the standards. In our fieldwork it is not surprising to find that teachers often harbor an initial resentment toward standards because they approach standards not as something that can guide their instruction, but rather as a top-down mandate they have been asked to comply with. This top-down directive often alienates teachers because their first reaction is that they are losing control of their ability to make professional decisions in the classroom. Obviously, when standards are viewed almost as a punitive measure, teachers quickly lose interest in working with them. Time should be spent having professional conversations about standards, their intent, the hurdles in implementing them, and how to overcome these hurdles while maintaining creative control in the classroom. We do not advocate that standards can or should be taught in the same way in every classroom. The teacher plays a significant role in determining how to deliver the standards to students in order to appeal to different interests, learning modalities, and readiness levels. The Strategic Design process merely becomes a vehicle for having conversations about these kinds of things, and teachers respect and appreciate the fact that they are treated as professionals and that their training, experience, and knowledge of their students' needs is honored.

The Strategic Design process, once executed in the classrooms, allows students to understand the "why" of what they are learning. One of the most significant outcomes of Strategic Design is that teachers design and deliver lessons that facilitate student understanding regarding why a particular subject, content, or skill is being taught in the classroom. If a teacher keeps this concept at the forefront of everything she or he does, then we truly believe that the attitudes and conversations that fill class-rooms will be much richer and deeper than those that result from the "I have to" or "because I said so" mentality.

Strategic Design provides concrete tools teachers can use to clarify what standards are and what they require students to know and be able to do at different grade levels and in different subjects. Teachers who are new to the profession have commented that they learned about the concept of "backward planning" in their credentialing programs, and they had initially thought that Strategic Design might be repetitious and a waste of their time. However, after experiencing the Strategic Design process first-hand, these same teachers would invariably comment that while they had learned about the concept of backward planning on a theoretical level, they had never learned how to actually apply the concept in their class-rooms, given the unique context each classroom presents. Once they have been exposed to Strategic Design, new and veteran teachers alike always say that they now feel empowered to actually develop lessons in a back-ward fashion.

Strategic Design aims to assist teachers in understanding how to use curricular resources in an effective, nimble manner. In utilizing Strategic Design, teachers may be wondering how to marry their district-adopted curricular program that is "standards aligned" with the Strategic Design process. It is important that teachers examine existing curricular programs they may have and actually work out a process of integrating Strategic Design with their existing programs. This is what makes this approach different: We are not just engaged in the application of a theoretical model, but perhaps more importantly, the applicability can be made specific to each teacher's needs. After utilizing the Strategic Design process, teach-ers can then utilize instructional materials in an "informed" manner. In other words, because the process provides such a comprehensive under-standing of the standards and a framework for approaching assessment and instructional strategies, teachers can then dig into curricular resources with an exact idea of what students will need to engage in the content and whether or not the curricular resource provides the right assessments and activities to facilitate mastery of content standards. Thus, teachers become critical consumers of instructional resources and will be enabled to determine exactly how, when, and why they can be most effectively utilized.

The Strategic Design process makes a lot of sense to educators because they feel it can make a material difference in their schools. But what we have learned over the years is that if we really want to effect positive change in education through the process, we have to help teachers actually use Strategic Design in relation to the unique set of variables that exist in their state, in their school district, and on their campus.

Now that we have previewed the role of Strategic Design in the teaching profession and highlighted a few of the benefits that can result from using this process, we would like to briefly describe how other authors have influenced our thinking.

INFLUENCE OF OTHER PROFESSIONALS IN THE FIELD

It does not take long to realize that our work has been heavily influenced by many of the relevant theories in the field. Thus, we felt it was important to acknowledge how these scholars informed our work. The following is a brief summary of the ways in which the important work being done in the field by some of the key researchers on classroom instruction has influenced us. The work of the people we discuss (and many others) is valuable in a variety of ways for the insight and guidance they have provided us as we evolved Strategic Design for Student Achievement. In the discussion that we present below, it is important for the reader to note that the overviews we present of the work of these great thinkers in the field of education is necessarily filtered through our lens. In other words, we have summarized *our* understanding (or interpretation) of their main theories. This discussion represents what we have taken away from each of these researchers as salient points to consider as we continue to develop and refine our own practices. We wholeheartedly acknowledge that there may be things we "missed" in their work or do not fully understand. Our objective in this section is not to critique their work, but rather to share with the reader how these researchers and practitioners have influenced our thinking and praxis.

Grant Wiggins and Jay McTighe—Understanding by Design (UbD)

Wiggins and McTighe are the authors who have most influenced our work and the development of Strategic Design. Strategic Design is based on the same overarching concept that Wiggins and McTighe used to develop Understanding by Design, what they have called "backward design." The term "backward design" has become quite well known in the field of education. Backward design makes a distinction between the function of teachers as deliverers of instruction versus those who are designers of instruction. Deliverers begin with textbooks, favored lessons, and time-honored activities, whereas designers derive these tools from targeted goals or standards. Backward design advocates that "one starts with the end—the desired results (goals or standards)—and then derives the curriculum from the evidence of learning (performances) called for by the standard and the teaching needed to equip students to perform" (Wiggins & McTighe, 1998, p. 8).

Perhaps the reason that we have been so drawn to the work of Wiggins and McTighe is that, like Strategic Design, Understanding by Design (UbD) is not a prescriptive program. Rather, both are conceptual frameworks. Neither UbD nor Strategic Design offer a specific curriculum, but rather ways to design or redesign any curriculum to make student understanding more likely. As teachers, we were immediately drawn to this concept. Strategic Design, like UbD, puts the power of curriculum design back in the hands of those closest to the students—teachers. We believe this is the best way to empower teachers to improve student achievement. However, we recognize that conceptually this can be overwhelming for teachers.

Although Strategic Design looks, on the surface, to be very similar to UbD, they are fundamentally different in their intent. Strategic Design is a standards-based instructional planning model. That is, it is completely reliant upon the use of standards. Strategic Design, as you will learn, is really a way to authentically embed standards into the planning process, and would not exist without standards. We have worked to provide a process for teachers to interact with the standards in a way that feels not only productive, but leads to an instructional program that moves students toward content mastery.

Strategic Design and UbD both utilize the same three stages that are involved in planning backward. However, the elements that comprise these three stages differ dramatically between UbD and Strategic Design. Wiggins and McTighe describe the three stages as follows: (1) identify desired results, (2) determine acceptable evidence, and (3) plan learning experiences and instruction. The Strategic Design process is also comprised of these three stages; however, we describe them differently because the steps involved in carrying out the three stages within Strategic Design differ in significant and conceptual ways from those inherent to the process outlined in UbD. In Strategic Design, the three stages are labeled as follows: (1) identify learning priorities, (2) align assessments, and (3) design instruction.

Richard Stiggins—Student-Involved Classroom Assessment

As we discuss in Chapter 3, the work of Richard Stiggins has played a critical role in the development of Strategic Design. We have always appreciated his straightforward approach to classroom assessment, which is why we have relied upon his work so heavily throughout our careers as teachers and consultants.

Today, standards-based reform efforts expect teachers to utilize assessment methods to assess student mastery of content knowledge specific to content standards. Both formative and summative assessment methods, aligned to content standards and classroom instruction, are used in classroom practice to inform teachers. What strikes a particular resonance for us is that in terms of Stiggins's work, *assessment is an instructional tool that promotes learning rather than an event designed solely for the purpose of evaluation and assigning grades* (Chappuis & Stiggins, 2002).

If you are familiar with Stiggins's work, you will probably recognize our classification of assessment methods (in Chapter 3) into selected response, constructed response, performance, and personal communication. Beginning with these classifications, Stiggins's process then assists teachers in identifying appropriate assessment methods through the use of Achievement Targets, namely knowledge, reasoning, skills, products, and dispositions. Stiggins's book, *Student-Involved Classroom Assessment, 3rd edition* (2001), emphasizes what teachers need to know to manage day-to-day classroom assessment effectively and efficiently; focuses on student well-being in assessment contexts, placing emphasis on student self-assessment; offers practical guidelines on how to construct all types of assessments; provides a unique explanation of how to match achievement targets to assessment methods; emphasizes time- and energy-saving ideas for teachers; and clearly relates the concepts in the book to traditional notions of validity and reliability.

While we philosophically agree with the approach utilized by Stiggins, we have departed from the use of Achievement Targets and use Bloom's taxonomy instead in our work to ensure appropriate alignment. Our goal in aligning assessments to standards is for teachers to think about what concrete, visible evidence students will produce to demonstrate mastery of the standard. The most direct link to find that appropriate evidence, in our opinion, is through Bloom's taxonomy. Additionally, since we spend so much time using Bloom's in the examination of content standards, it only makes sense that we continue using this tool to ensure that the entire instructional design program is effectively aligned. The foundation of our model is the examination of the levels of thinking required by the standards in order to ensure student success. By also aligning assessments to the standards using Bloom's, we are able to ensure a tight alignment.

As you may have gathered from our words here and the book in general, we do not believe that comparisons between one scholar, or researcher, or approach, and another is particularly valuable. In the best learning environment, we should always be able to find what is valuable to us, and build on that value to individualize it for our purposes. Similarly, we do not believe that any aspect of Strategic Design essentially conflicts with the work of Stiggins. Rather, we believe that Strategic Design can effectively provide the foundation within which the processes developed by Stiggins can be employed, and the full benefit of Stiggins's work can be realized.

Robert J. Marzano, Debra J. Pickering, and Jane E. Pollock—*Classroom Instruction That Works*

Classroom Instruction That Works (2001) has become one of the most referenced resources in relation to increasing student achievement. In this book, Marzano, Pickering, and Pollock describe nine instructional strategies that are proven to increase student achievement. The authors describe how their motivation for writing such a book stemmed from recent research that has shown that an "individual teacher can have a powerful effect on her students even *if the school doesn't*" (Marzano, Pickering, & Pollock, 2001, p. 2, emphasis in original). Along with this statement comes dramatic implications for increasing student achievement. "If we can identify what those highly effective teachers do, then even more of the differences in student achievement can be accounted for" (Marzano, Pickering, & Pollock, 2001, p. 3). All of this, combined with the research that demonstrates that the most important factor affecting student achievement is the teacher, has ignited the idea that if we can just identify the strategies that good teachers utilize in their classrooms and make a conscious effort to use these strategies, then we can have a profound, positive effect on student achievement. Therefore, Marzano, Pickering, and Pollock conducted a meta-analysis of instructional strategies used by teachers and distilled the results into nine broad teaching strategies that have positive effects on student learning. The strategies are: identifying similarities and differences; summarizing and note-taking; reinforcing effort and providing recognition; homework and practice; nonlinguistic representations; cooperative learning; setting objectives and providing feedback; generating and testing hypotheses; questions, cues, and advance organizers.

Strategic Design acknowledges the power of this research and these instructional strategies and encourages teachers to use such strategies.

However, as stated earlier in our discussion on Wiggins and McTighe, Strategic Design places a premium on considering the context in which these strategies are used by teachers in the classroom. Strategic Design assumes that these strategies may be useful in facilitating student learning. However, if that student learning is not directed toward a specific outcome, then the time spent using these strategies in the classroom is wasted. The learning priority (standards) must be identified and clarified first, before a strategy can be chosen that would best suit the purpose of teaching to that learning priority. Unless a teacher has fully analyzed the standards and identified the level of thinking (Bloom's) a standard requires, it is quite possible that a teacher might use one of the nine teaching strategies to promote a level of thinking among students that is inconsistent with the level of thinking required by a standard. For example, one of the nine strategies is homework and practice. Unless a teacher identifies the purpose of the homework and what type of skills students should practice, then this strategy could very well turn into nothing more than busywork for students. In fact, homework and practice is often misused or misconstrued as busywork because the learning priority has not been clearly identified by the teacher and communicated to students. Any time homework and practice is assigned, it should be clear to all (teacher, students, parents) how the homework will allow the student an opportunity to gain facility in the types of skills or knowledge that will be needed to do well on the assessment and demonstrate mastery of the learning priority (standards). The third stage of the Strategic Design process helps teachers analyze teaching strategies in relation to the context within which they are to be used in order to help teachers make good decisions about how to use strategies effectively.

CHAPTER 2

Stage One:
Prioritizing and
Clustering Standards

One of the very real difficulties in teaching in a standards-based system, in which there are seemingly a multitude of standards that must be addressed as part of our core instructional program within the course of an academic year, is that it often feels as if we are faced with an impossible task. Our goal in this chapter is to render the task of teaching standards more manageable and meaningful through the engagement of the prioritization and clustering process that we describe in detail below. Prioritization allows for a clear conceptual understanding of the standard, and provides a way to teach the standard in a manner that enables precise, relevant, and effective instruction. Clustering assists teachers in grouping standards to enable instruction on multiple concepts within the same unit or lesson. These discrete but critically aligned processes of prioritizing and clustering standards allow the teacher to streamline the instructional design process and provide units of instruction that address the inherent complexity of standards while designing and delivering lessons that are precisely targeted to the standards, and are also engaging at the same time.

Through the application of the Strategic Design process, educators are empowered to make informed decisions about how to meaningfully and appropriately address standards in their grade level(s) and subject area(s). The Standards Analysis and Prioritization Flow Chart presented in this chapter (Figure 2.1) is designed to facilitate the decisionmaking process, particularly when done in collaboration with colleagues, regarding the prioritization of content standards. In some cases, the prioritization process validates our thinking about how we treat certain standards. In other cases, this process challenges our thinking about how we had previously addressed standards or will address them in the future.

While the flow chart provides both a schematic outline and a certain level of objectivity, it is vital to remember that prioritizing standards is a *process*. Thus, definitionally the term implies that there will be instances when there are no clear right or wrong answers. In such cases, collaboration with colleagues can be helpful in order to deeply examine standards and ultimately reach a better understanding regarding the levels of priority to be assigned. The process-oriented nature of prioritizing standards also implies that once standards have been prioritized, they should be revisited from time to time to account for new understandings that surface as a result of teaching the standards over time.

BENEFITS OF PRIORITIZING STANDARDS

Deep Understanding of Content

Educators gain a deep understanding of content standards by engaging in concrete steps that ultimately result in the prioritization and clustering of the standards. This is one of the most valuable aspects of this stage of Strategic Design. We truly believe that a deeper understanding of content standards is as valuable as the product (prioritized standards) that teachers walk away with at the end of the process. This deep understanding serves as a critical foundation for the rest of the process and enables teachers to concretize standards in a material way. Because the process of prioritizing standards is collaborative by nature, teachers have the added benefit of validating their own understanding of content and clarifying any misconceptions they may have had about the standards. Thus, teachers are able to calibrate their thinking about what the standards are asking of their students.

As we have been pointing out through the course of this book, Strategic Design places a high premium on teacher control of curriculum. We are aware, through our own experiences, as well as through the evidence of current research, that teachers are the variable that has the greatest impact on student achievement. Teachers are in a position to design, adjust, deliver, and monitor content in ways that best serve their unique students. In order to maintain this critical pedagogical flexibility in a system in which a prescribed set of standards serves as the foundation for accountability, teachers must deeply understand the content and skills embedded in standards.

Greater Sense of Direction

Teachers report that they have a better sense of direction regarding how to teach the standards after going through the prioritization process.

Instructional guidance occurs once teachers identify those standards that will serve as anchors for units. This central focus helps teachers allocate instructional time and resources effectively. As teachers begin to shape units of instruction, they start with the central focus, which helps teachers develop themes for units and build connections to other standards within and outside the same content area.

Relevance to Teaching and Learning

Once the central focus within standards has been identified, teachers are able to design instruction around this focus. The importance of this instruction can go beyond the specificity of mastering the standards themselves, since by demonstrating future practical application of the standards, students feel that what they are learning is more relevant than merely taking in information that is unrelated to them. In addition, teachers can then shape instruction of other related standards around the focus standards. If students can see a connection between a discrete skill or piece of knowledge that they are learning and an overarching concept, and understand how that information supports or relates to an overarching concept, they are much more likely to be engaged in the learning because they see relevance in what they are being asked to learn. A critical element that defines high-quality instruction is that students feel connected to what they are learning in multiple ways: academically, personally, and as learners. Overarching concepts help create a bridge between the content students are learning and their connections to that content.

Analyzing standards serves as a prerequisite to aligning assessments to standards and choosing appropriate instructional strategies for day-to-day classroom instruction. Instead of just telling teachers that they need to "teach to the standards," the Strategic Design process gives teachers the tools that effectively enable them to do so.

The analyses of standards that take place in Stage One of the process helps teachers decide how to most effectively and efficiently assess and instruct to each of the standards. Specifically, teachers should design assessments that incorporate the correlative level of thinking, as required by Bloom's Taxonomy, that is implied by the standards. Subsequently, the instructional activities chosen should provide students with opportunities to acquire the knowledge and practice the skills required by the standards. This concept of aligning assessments and instruction to standards will be explored in greater detail in subsequent chapters. Suffice it to say that the analysis of standards serves as a foundation for this alignment to take place.

STAGE ONE OF THE STRATEGIC DESIGN PROCESS

Analyzing and Prioritizing Content Standards

If we expect standards to drive curricular decisionmaking, it is imperative that teachers have a structured process by which to analyze standards. Stage One of Strategic Design provides such a structure. As teachers examine the standards more deeply using the process detailed in this chapter, they learn to prioritize standards into three categories; Priority 1 (P1), Priority 2 (P2), and Priority 3 (P3). The prioritization process enables teachers to identify essential skills and knowledge elements that are embedded in standards. There are several important reasons for engaging in this prioritization process:

1. Teachers must deeply understand the content they are teaching in order to design curriculum around that content.
2. Curriculum content must be organized in a way that maintains a consistent focus on the overarching concepts contained in the standards.
3. Teachers must be strategic about addressing all content relevant to achieving proficiency in the established standards within the course of a year.

Prioritizing is not about deciding which standards are the most important and then eliminating some standards from the curriculum. Rather, it is about organizing them in a way that maintains a consistent focus on the overarching concepts.

So how does a teacher begin to make distinctions between the overarching concepts and those concepts or skills embedded in the standard that support multifaceted, complex concepts? These distinctions are made by assigning a priority to each of the standards.

The prioritization process asks teachers to apply a specific criterion and ask key questions of each of the standards to determine which of the standards represent Priority 1 (P1), Priority 2 (P2), and Priority 3 (P3) types of thinking and skills. We have organized the criterion that needs to be utilized during the prioritization process in Figure 2.1 in order to provide some direction and structure. Based on focus groups and our experience utilizing this process with teachers in their classrooms across the country, we have created and refined a step-by-step flow chart that contains objective criteria and key questions to help teachers analyze and prioritize the standards.

FIGURE 2.1. **Standards Analysis and Prioritization Flow Chart**

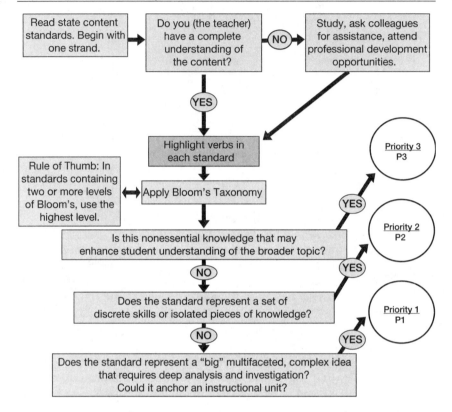

The remainder of this chapter is dedicated to providing a thorough explanation and modeling of the flow chart. It is important to note that initially the flow chart is meant to be used as a guiding tool for shaping a teacher's thinking about standards. It is our expectation that eventually, as teachers repeatedly engage in the process of closely examining standards, the flow chart will not be necessary because the concepts contained therein will have been internalized. The set of standards presented in Figure 2.2 will be utilized as examples of how to concretely apply this process.

Step One—Reading the Standards

As indicated in the Standards Analysis and Prioritization Flow Chart, Step One is to read the state content standards. As basic as this may sound, since the analysis process requires teachers to make distinctions between standards, the logical first step is to preview all of the standards in order get a sense of the entire scope of skills and knowledge elements they

FIGURE 2.2. Sample History/Social Science Standards

Grade 5 History/Social Science
American Revolution

Standard 1: Determine the causes of the American Revolution and analyze its consequences.

Standard 2: Identify and map the major military battles, campaigns, and turning points of the Revolutionary War.

Standard 3: Identify the different roles women played during the Revolution.

Standard 4: Identify and compare the contributions of France and other nations and of individuals to the outcome of the Revolution.

embody. This careful first reading enables us to compare one standard against another. For multisubject or multigrade teachers, we recommend beginning the process with one subject area or one grade level.

When reading the standards, teachers should begin to get a sense for both the content listed in the standard (often contained in the nouns) and the skills listed in the standard (often contained in the verbs). Also, it is important to be aware of the multiple concepts embedded in a standard. Standards are often complex and packed with information; therefore, this process is designed to enable teachers to disentangle these concepts, which is necessary in order to be able to prioritize the standards, make connections between standards, and ultimately choose appropriate assessments and instructional activities for the standards. As we read to try to decipher the language within the standard, we have to try to grasp the central concept that the standard represents and incorporates. At this point, it may be useful to write a few notes while reading the standards, as the note-taking may facilitate a deeper analysis of the standards. It is also important during this reading to constantly refer back to the central idea a standard represents and what it is trying to convey.

When reading the standards, being cognizant of the organizational structure of the standards enables a more complete understanding of the document, and can help focus our analysis and prioritization on the most discrete learning outcomes contained in the standard. Since the format and structure for the organization of standards varies from state to state, it would be impossible to provide a single example of what this initial reading and analytical process might look like. Despite these variances, what is most important is that teachers must focus on the most discrete learning objectives contained in the standard. Often standards are listed within a larger "set" or context that is delineated or labeled above the standard itself. For example, the standard presented in Figure 2.3 is taken from the California English/Language Arts standards (California Department of Education, 2007). These standards are organized using a four-tiered system.

Figure 2.3. Standards Organizational Structure

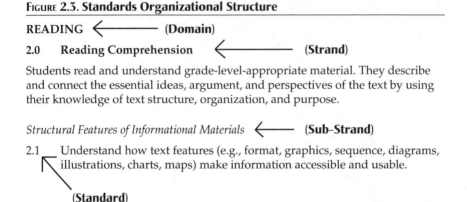

READING ←———— (Domain)

2.0   Reading Comprehension   ←————   (Strand)

Students read and understand grade-level-appropriate material. They describe and connect the essential ideas, argument, and perspectives of the text by using their knowledge of text structure, organization, and purpose.

Structural Features of Informational Materials ←—— (**Sub-Strand**)

2.1   Understand how text features (e.g., format, graphics, sequence, diagrams, illustrations, charts, maps) make information accessible and usable.

   (**Standard**)

Domain. The first tier of the standards document is the domain. California English/Language Arts standards are organized into four domains: (1) Reading, (2) Writing, (3) Written and Oral Language Conventions, and (4) Listening and Speaking. The example above shows that Standard 2.1 falls within the Reading domain. The domain represents the broadest tier of skill or knowledge element that the standard represents.

Strand. The next tier is the strand. Standard 2.1 falls under the Reading Comprehension strand. You will notice that there is a description of the strand just below the strand title. This description helps build context for the standards that follow.

Sub-Strand. The third tier is called the sub-strand, which provides an even narrower context for the standard that follows. Standard 2.1 falls under the Structural Features of Informational Materials sub-strand.

Standard. Finally, we arrive at the standard—in this example, the most discrete learning objective. In reading the sample standard in Figure 2.3, it is referring to a student's reading abilities (domain). More specifically, it is referring to a student's ability to read and understand grade-level-appropriate material (strand). And even more specifically, the standard will contain some type of content or skills related to a student's ability to use structural features of informational material (sub-strand) to read and understand grade-level-appropriate material.

Although the standards in a given state may not be organized like those in California, the process provided in this book can still be easily applied regardless of format variances from state to state. When making decisions regarding the prioritization of standards, we are asking teachers to prioritize the most specific desired learning outcomes described in the document. In some states these learning outcomes are referred to as the standards; in others, the learning outcomes are called the performance standards, grade-level expectations, assessment objectives, benchmarks, or performance outcomes, to name a few. Regardless of what they are called, it is important to identify the most specific learning objectives contained in the standards document because ultimately we want to build units and lessons around the most specific objectives. Therefore, when examining standards, it is important to be aware of the organizational structure that is used and be able to identify the most specific learning objectives embedded within that structure—what, exactly, do students need to know and/or be able to do?

Step Two—Examining Your Own Understanding of the Content

Step Two asks teachers to look at the standards individually and determine whether or not they have a complete understanding of the content or skills the standards describe. This is a critically important part of the prioritization process, as a thorough and complete understanding of the content of the standard will subsequently impact our instructional strategies and all aspects of actually teaching the skills and knowledge required by the standard. While the following may seem self-evident, because teachers are sometimes required to teach in an unfamiliar grade level, particularly in elementary schools, it is necessary to inventory one's own knowledge of the content and skills required by the standards at the new grade level in order to effectively design and deliver standards-based lessons for students. Also, there are times when a teacher may in fact be teaching a grade level or subject area that is familiar, however, the content described in the standard is so broad or the language is sufficiently unclear that despite the teacher's expertise or experience with the subject matter, the text requires some clarification about what the standard is really asking the student to know and be able to do. For example, in Standard 2 in Figure 2.2, you may be unfamiliar with the major military battles, campaigns, or turning points of the Revolutionary War. It may be necessary for the teacher to refresh his or her own knowledge of the American Revolution in order to feel comfortable analyzing and prioritizing this standard in relation to other standards. If teachers do not have a complete understanding of the content and skills being described by the standard, they should take time to fill in any gaps in their own knowledge by studying, asking colleagues for assistance, or attending professional development on relevant topics.

If further clarification is needed on a concept contained in the standards, it is often helpful to go to the particular state's Department of Education Web site and search for companion documents relevant to the standards. Often states produce frameworks that describe the standards in greater detail and demonstrate sample standards-based units. Usually the Department of Education will suggest other resources, particularly Web-based resources, to help teachers in the implementation of standards. Most supplemental documents that have been generated to facilitate a better understanding of the standards have been derived from previous iterations of specific learning objectives articulated by content-specific national organizations such as the National Council for Teachers of Mathematics (NCTM) or the International Reading Association (IRA). It may be helpful to search internet resources that such organizations provide as well.

Step Three—Highlighting Verbs and Applying Bloom's Taxonomy

Once a teacher feels confident that they have a solid understanding of the content and skills described by the standard, the next step is to highlight the verbs in the standards (see Figure 2.4).

The verbs in the standards describe what a student is expected to do and/or the type of thinking required by a student in order to successfully learn the content outlined in the standard. Highlighting the verbs draws the teacher's attention to the skills and knowledge elements included in the standards and facilitates the application of Bloom's taxonomy (Bloom, 1956) to the standards. Bloom's taxonomy serves as the classificatory system we use to categorize the type of thinking required by the standards. There are key words associated with each level of thinking as outlined by Bloom; these key words are typically verbs. Therefore, by highlighting the verbs in the standards, teachers can align the verbs to the key words

---

FIGURE 2.4. Sample History/Social Science Standards with Highlighted Verbs

**Grade 5 History/Social Science
American Revolution**

Standard 1: **Determine** the causes of the American Revolution and **analyze** its consequences.

Standard 2: **Identify** and **map** the major military battles, campaigns, and turning points of the Revolutionary War.

Standard 3: **Identify** the different roles women played during the Revolution.

Standard 4: **Identify** and **compare** the contributions of France and other nations and of individuals to the outcome of the Revolution.

---

in Bloom's in order to begin the conversation about the level of cognition each standard represents.

Step Four—Aligning the "Levels of Thinking" in Bloom's to the Standards

Next, we will apply the six levels of thinking represented by Bloom's taxonomy to the standards (see Figure 2.5).

At this point in the process, teachers determine the level of thinking (as outlined in Bloom's) that each standard requires of a student. We do this for several reasons. First, in order to attach a level of thinking to each standard, teachers must determine exactly what the standard requires students to do. The verbs in the standard serve as a starting point for the analysis, since they can be aligned to the key words listed for each level in Bloom's taxonomy.

We use Bloom's to facilitate a deeper, more objective analysis of standards. In this sense, Bloom's serves as a catalyst for analyzing standards. As a result of applying Bloom's taxonomy, standards become clearer not only for each individual teacher, but also for the collective group responsible for teaching the standard.

Since the critical task at hand is to correlate the standards to the levels of thinking in Bloom's taxonomy, being attentive to the specific language of the standards, as well as of the taxonomy, is critical. As a result, it is important to note that there are some caveats that accompany the task of finding a correspondence between the verbs in the standards and the key words in Bloom's six levels of thinking. Reexamining the standards for the American Revolution (see Figure 2.4) will enable us to explore the kinds of judgment calls we have to make when we encounter these nuances in the process.

Key words are sometimes found in more than one level of Bloom's. Let's look at the verb *identify*, which is often used when writing standards. When comparing the verb *identify* to the key words in Bloom's, we see that *identify* is listed in both Level I (knowledge) as well as Level III (application). When this occurs it is helpful to *look at the definition for each level in Bloom's* in order to make a decision regarding what level the verb really belongs to. In such a case, we could ask ourselves if the standards are asking students to merely access their memory of previously learned material by recalling facts, terms, basic concepts, and answers (knowledge), or do the standards require students to solve problems by applying acquired knowledge to new situations, facts, techniques, and rules in a different way?

Let's look back at our sample standards for the American Revolution to solidify this concept. In Standard 2, the verb *identify* simply asks students

FIGURE 2.5. Bloom's Taxonomy

Level I: Knowledge

Exhibit memory of previously learned material by recalling facts, terms, basic concepts, and answers.

KEY WORDS: choose · define · describe · find · how · identify · label · list · match · name · recall · relate · select · show · spell · tell

Level II: Comprehension

Demonstrate understanding of facts and ideas by organizing, comparing, translating, interpreting, giving descriptions, and stating main ideas.

KEY WORDS: classify · compare · contrast · demonstrate · explain · extend · illustrate · indicate · infer · interpret · outline · relate · rephrase · summarize · show · tell · translate

Level III: Application

Solve problems to new situations by applying acquired knowledge, facts, techniques, and rules in a different way.

KEY WORDS: apply · build · choose · construct · develop · experiment with · explain · identify · interview · make use of · model · organize · plan · select · solve · utilize

Level IV: Analysis

Examine and break information into parts by identifying motives or causes. Make inferences and find evidence to support generalizations.

KEY WORDS: analyze · categorize · compare · contrast · discover · dissect · distinguish · divide · examine · function inspect · list · simplify · survey · take part in · test for

Level V: Synthesis

Compile information together in a different way by combining elements in a new pattern or proposing alternative solutions.

KEY WORDS: adapt · build · change · choose · combine · compile · compose · construct · create · design · develop · discuss · elaborate · estimate · formulate · imagine · improve · invent · make up · minimize · modify · originate · plan · predict · propose · solve · suppose · theorize

Level VI: Evaluation

Present and defend opinions by making judgments about information, validity of ideas, or quality of work based on a set of criteria.

KEY WORDS: appraise · assess · award · choose · compare · conclude · criticize · decide · deduct · defend · determine · dispute · evaluate · explain · interpret · judge · justify · mark · measure · perceive · prioritize · prove · rate · recommend · rule · select · value to *recall* the major military battles of the Revolutionary War. The standard does not ask students to *apply* their knowledge of the major battles to another unique or disparate situation. Therefore, we believe the verb *identify* in this standard represents Level I (knowledge) on Bloom's taxonomy. Similarly, in Standard 3, the verb *identify* simply asks students to recognize the different roles women played in the war. The standard does not require students to *use* their knowledge of the roles women played to *create* or *develop* a case study of the evolution of women's roles throughout history, for example. Therefore, the verb *identify* in Standard 3 also represents Level I (knowledge) on Bloom's taxonomy. By contrast, in Standard 4, the verb *identify* requires students to *develop* or *use* their knowledge of the contributions made by France, other nations, and individuals to the war in order to understand the relative value of each of these contributions as they relate to the outcome of the war. Clearly, the verb *identify* in this case requires a much deeper level of thinking from students; therefore, it is classified as Level III (application) on Bloom's taxonomy because students are applying their knowledge to develop a deeper understanding of the outcomes of the war.

This type of exercise in clarification leads to productive conversations regarding what standards actually require of a student. This clarity would then impact the way we both assess and instruct toward fulfilling the requirements inherent to that standard.

Some standards have multiple levels of Bloom's within them. Looking at Standard 4, for example, we see that the two verbs (*identify* and *compare*) would be classified at different levels within Bloom's taxonomy. The term *identify*, in this case, is probably Level III (application), while *compare* is likely to be Level IV (analysis). When this occurs, teachers should list all levels in Bloom's that are applicable to the standard, and account for both levels in the prioritization process. This is a clear example of how standards sometimes pack a great deal of information and skill requirements into one phrase. Discerning the two different levels tells us that in this case, students will be required to *use* knowledge to *analyze* the contributions of France, other nations, and individuals in relation to the outcome of the war. This has implications for how we assess and choose instructional activities to teach this standard.

The list of key words provided in this chapter is not an exhaustive list. There may be several other verbs found in standards that are not listed in Figure 2.5. If a standard contains a verb not found on the key words list, it is helpful to think of a synonym for the verb that may be similar to one of the key words listed. For example, the verb *use* is sometimes found in standards. A synonym for *use* may be *utilize*, which is listed in Level III (application) of Bloom's taxonomy. The definition for each level of Bloom's can be helpful when this occurs.

Some standards do not contain clearly articulated verbs that correspond to Bloom's taxonomy. It is important to note that some standards do not contain clearly articulated verbs that correspond or correlate with Bloom's taxonomy. For example, the science content standards shown in Figure 2.6 all use the verb *know*.

The verb *know* can have many different levels of thinking that obtain with reference to it, depending on the context in which the verb is used. Therefore, it is important to look at the other words in the standard to more specifically discern the type of thinking the standard requires. In the science standards above, we can enhance and clarify the verb *know* (since it is not particularly helpful in our analysis) by focusing on the words *distinguish* and *construct*. Thus it is possible to assign a level of Bloom's taxonomy to each of these standards, which provides more clarity regarding what the standards are really asking the student to do. It is more helpful to think about students having to "distinguish" and "construct" something rather than just "know" something. "Distinguish" and "construct" are more exact terms that help us assign a level of thinking to the standard, whereas the verb "know" often has more liminal implications, and in this instance is not helpful to our endeavors. Determining the level of thinking required by standards at this stage in the Strategic Design process serves as a prerequisite to designing assessments and instructional activities aligned to the same level of thinking required by the standard.

Up to this point in our discussion about assigning a level of Bloom's to standards, we have presented examples of what this looks like via most of our sample standards (Figure 2.4—Grade 5, History/Social Science, American Revolution). As a way of providing closure to this discussion, we felt it would be useful to provide a short summary of our thinking regarding the level of Bloom's we would assign to the verbs in all of the sample standards, those previously discussed, as well as Standard 1, which has not yet been addressed. Figure 2.7 represents this summary.

Figure 2.6. Sample Science Standards

Science Standards, Grade 5

- Students **know** the characteristics that <u>distinguish</u> plant cells from animal cells, including chloroplasts and cell walls.
- Students **know** how to <u>construct</u> a simple branching diagram to classify living groups of organisms by shared derived characteristics.

Figure 2.7. Assigning Bloom's Taxonomy to Sample Standards

Standard	Verbs	Bloom's Level	Rationale
Determine the causes of the American Revolution	*Determine*	Level IV—Analysis	Students must find causes and motives of the war, which is inherent in the definition of analysis.
and *analyze* its consequences.	*Analyze*	Level IV—Analysis	Analyze = analysis.
Identify and *map* the major military battles, campaigns, and turning points of the Revolutionary War.	*Identify*	Level I—Knowledge	Asks students to simply recall the major military battles.
	Map	Level I—Knowledge	Students are asked to *label* the location of the battles. Labeling only requires identifying the geographic location of the battles on a map, which represents simple recall of these locations.
Identify the different roles women played during the Revolution.	*Identify*	Level I—Knowledge	The standard asks students to simply recognize roles women played. This could be as simple as listing the various roles. Listing roles represents simple recall, which is a function of Level I—Knowledge.
Identify and *compare* the contributions of France and other nations and of individuals to the outcome of the Revolution.	*Identify*	Level III—Application	Requires students to *develop* or *use* their knowledge of the various contributions of countries and individuals to help understand the outcome of the Revolution.
	Compare	Level IV—Analysis	Students must make *inferences* regarding how the contributions various countries and people made to the war affected the outcome of the war. Making inferences is inherent in the definition of analysis.

Step Five—Key Questions

At this point in the process, a significant amount of analysis of the standards has already occurred. Now it is time to fine-tune this analysis and ultimately prioritize standards as Priority 1 (P1), Priority 2 (P2), or Priority 3 (P3). To do this, the content and the language of the standards are filtered, one at a time, through a series of key questions contained in Step Five.

> *Key Question 1*: Does the standard represent nonessential knowledge that nevertheless may enhance student understanding of the topic?
> *Key Question 2*: Does the standard represent discrete skills or isolated pieces of knowledge?
> *Key Question 3*: Does the standard represent a multifaceted, complex idea that requires deep analysis and investigation?

The wording of the three questions has been chosen carefully so as to align to the criteria for ultimately prioritizing standards as P1, P2, or P3. Key Question 1 is aligned to a P3 classification, Key Question 2 is aligned to a P2 classification, and Key Question 3 is aligned to a P1 classification (as depicted in Figure 2.1). The order of the questions is also significant. As teachers filter standards through each of the questions, they are quite literally trying to make a case for P1 classification of a standard. Each of the questions represents criteria that help us interpret standards and make distinctions between them. In doing so we are not only comparing standards to the key questions, we are inherently comparing standards against one another. (It is important to remind the reader once again that we are not advocating the complete dismissal of any standards. Rather, the prioritization process and the criteria for selecting a P1, P2, or P3 standard are designed to enable teachers to find standards that represent multifaceted, complex ideas, so that they can organize other standards around these ideas.) The key questions help us make such distinctions.

Key Question 1 is asking if a standard represents nonessential knowledge that may nevertheless enhance a student's understanding of the topic. Nonessential knowledge is information that if forgotten by a student after he or she leaves the classroom would still allow him or her to understand the core ideas related to the topic. These standards are classified as Priority 3 (P3) standards.

Key Question 2 assumes that the standard is essential to the topic, but that the knowledge or skills described within the standard are discrete or isolated. Discrete skills or isolated pieces of knowledge are skills that do not require extensive investigation or analysis in order to understand them. More often than not, these standards serve as the prerequisite knowledge required in order for students to understand the more complex standards. If the standard is an isolated skill or piece of knowledge, the standard is classified as a Priority 2 (P2) standard.

By contrast, the third and final question of the flow chart asks the teacher to determine if the standard being examined represents a multi-faceted, complex idea that requires deep investigation. If the standard is a complex concept that requires this type of analysis and investigation, the standard is classified as a Priority 1 (P1) standard.

When considering each of these key questions, many find it helpful to work collaboratively (e.g., as a grade level or department) in order to voice multiple opinions and ultimately reach a consensus. Let us revisit our American Revolution standards to concretize the application of the key questions. To do this we will filter each standard through the key questions and assign a priority to each of the standards. Additionally, we will provide a rationale for the priority assigned to each standard so that the reader can get a sense of what the thinking and conversation among teachers might look like when they engage in the process.

While reading through these examples, it is imperative to keep in mind that the rationale presented for our prioritization of these sample standards is not *the* rationale. Remember, Strategic Design is a process that provides teachers with the opportunity to make professional judgments about their curriculum; specifically, in this case, the prioritization of standards. Therefore, what is presented below is our professional judgment of these standards given the key questions that helped us inform our rationale for prioritization. The key questions are meant to inform our decisions and provide a forum for discussing our interpretations of the standards. And we believe the key questions are very effective in accomplishing this. However, there is not always a clear right or wrong answer to the key questions or the way you might prioritize standards. This is one very clear example of why we call Strategic Design a process and not a predesigned program. It is meant to encourage critical thinking and dialogue in order to clarify the way we teach and assess standards. Teachers have often asked us to "tell them" the right answer when prioritizing. Strategic Design is not about giving the right answers to teachers. Rather, we consider ourselves facilitators of conversations that promote a deeper understanding of standards, thus enabling teachers to be more effective and creative in the way they teach standards in the classroom.

Below is our interpretation and prioritization of the American Revolution standards presented in Figure 2.2 via the key questions.

Standard 1: *Determine the causes of the American Revolution and analyze its consequences.*

> *Key Question 1:* Is this standard nonessential knowledge that nevertheless may enhance student understanding of the topic?
> *Answer:* No.

This standard represents something that we want students to remember long after they leave the classroom. Without an understanding of the causes and the consequences of the American Revolution, students will be left with little, if any, understanding of the topic. Therefore, this standard is more than nonessential. It is not a P3 standard and we continue with the prioritization process.

> *Key Question 2:* Does the standard represent discrete skills or isolated pieces of knowledge?
> *Answer:* No.

There are multiple factors and numerous pieces of knowledge that students must consider in order to demonstrate an understanding of the causes and consequences of the war. Therefore the standard does not represent discrete skills or isolated pieces of knowledge, and it is not a P2 standard.

> *Key Question 3:* Does the standard represent a multifaceted, complex idea that requires deep analysis and investigation?
> *Answer:* Yes.

Cause and effect of war is a multifaceted, complex concept as evidenced, in part, by the level of thinking this standard requires of students. The causes and consequences are the overarching concepts students should be able to articulate when discussing the American Revolution. Notice that the verbs used in this standard, *determine* and *analyze* represent higher levels of thinking on Bloom's taxonomy as well, further confirming that this standard represents a multifaceted, complex idea that requires higher levels of thinking. A P1 standard often represents the culmination of several skills or discrete pieces of content. It will likely require students to use the skills or content knowledge they have acquired in new or unique ways. It is easy to connect discrete pieces of knowledge (e.g., battles, dates, people involved) to the causes and consequences of war; therefore, this could quite easily serve as an anchor for a unit with multiple standards attached to it. These are the types of standards that serve as good P1s. Additionally, causes and consequences of war are universal concepts that can be analyzed in relation to *any* war, not just the American Revolution. Therefore, this standard meets the definition of a multifaceted concept, rather than a discrete or nonessential piece of knowledge, and is prioritized as P1.

Standard 2: *Identify and map the major military battles, campaigns, and turning points of the Revolutionary War.*

> *Key Question 1*: Is this standard nonessential knowledge that nevertheless may enhance student understanding of the topic?
> *Answer*: No.

Knowledge of the major military battles and campaigns and where they occurred is more than nonessential knowledge, especially in reference to the major turning points of the Revolutionary War. Without understanding the major battles, campaigns, and turning points of the war and their geographic locations, it would be impossible for a student to fully articulate the results and consequences of the war. Therefore, the answer to this key question is "no." This standard is not a P3, and we continue with the prioritization process.

> *Key Question 2*: Does the standard represent discrete skills or isolated pieces of knowledge?
> *Answer*: Yes.

Knowing the battles and the turning points of the war is essential knowledge, yet it does not rise to the level of a multifaceted, complex concept the way Standard 1 does. This standard simply requires memorization and recall, rather than reasoning, inference, and evaluation. This standard could easily be taught as part and parcel of the causes and consequences of the American Revolution, but the unit would not revolve around the major military battles. In contrast, the unit could easily revolve around Standard 1, the causes and consequences of the war. Therefore, the answer to question two is "yes"; the major battles, campaigns, and turning points of the war are isolated facts that we would teach in relation to a broader concept such as the causes and consequences of the war. Because the answer to this question is "yes," the prioritization of this standard is complete. It is a P2 standard.

Standard 3: *Identify the different roles women played during the Revolution.*

> *Key Question 1*: Is this standard nonessential knowledge that nevertheless may enhance student understanding of the topic?
> *Answer*: Yes.

Standard 3 appears to be nonessential to mastering the key concepts of the American Revolution; however, it may enhance a student's understanding of the topic. It is plausible that if students were unable to identify the different roles women played during the Revolution, they might still be able to grasp the larger concepts regarding the Revolutionary War, such as the causes and consequences. However, information regarding the roles women played during the American Revolution may help some students better access the key concepts, and do so in a more complete way. One can certainly argue that the role of women during the Revolution can be connected to the broader concepts that form the overarching concept about the American Revolution that we want students to successfully master. Remember that one of the primary goals of the prioritization process is to identify those standards that will serve as the focal point for instruction. In this case, we have determined that the focal point will be the causes and consequences of the war. Therefore, the answer to Key Question 1 is "yes"; this is a P3 standard, and the prioritization process ends here for this standard.

Standard 4: *Identify and compare the contributions of France and other nations and of individuals to the outcome of the Revolution.*

Key Question 1: Is this standard nonessential knowledge that nevertheless may enhance student understanding of the topic?
Answer: No.

The contributions that France, other nations, and individuals made to the war are more than nonessential pieces of knowledge, particularly in relation to the outcome of the Revolution. Because the contributions of these various nations have a direct impact on outcome of the war, knowing them becomes essential. Therefore, the answer to key question one is "no"; this is not a P3 standard and we move on to Key Question 2.

Key Question 2: Does the standard represent discrete skills or isolated pieces of knowledge?
Answer: Yes.

While the contributions that France, other nations, and individuals made to the outcome of the war feel like a large concept, we compared these concepts to Standard 1, which focuses on the causes and consequences of the war. Once again, the causes and consequences represent the larger, more complex idea when comparing all of these standards, and we would teach about the contributions of France, other nations, and individuals in relation to the causes and consequences. Therefore, we prioritized this standard as a P2, isolated pieces of knowledge that could and should be discussed in relation standard one. The prioritization process ends here for this standard.

It is important to note that one of the key determinants for how we prioritized this standard was its relationship to other standards. Looking at this standard in isolation, one could easily make the case that it might be a P1. However, comparing this standard to the others in the sample helped us define the concept of a discrete skill or isolated piece of knowledge (criteria for a P2) and distinguish this concept from a multifaceted, complex idea (criteria for a P1).

You will find that as you start to internalize the standards more deeply through this process, connections between standards arise that may cause you to change an initial prioritization. Making such changes is actually a sign of productive engagement with the process; in fact, such changes should be expected. Remember, Strategic Design is a process, which implies that it is ongoing and evolves and functions differently as we get better at it and/or upon receiving new information. The process is constructed in such a way that it values and respects teachers as growing professionals, and encourages independent thinking on their part. Strategic Design embraces changes once units or lessons are taught and new discoveries are made regarding the standards. Indeed, it is important to remain open to the way the prioritization process evolves every time it is utilized.

While prioritizing some of the standards can be fairly easy or obvious, utilizing the three key questions we have presented, there is likely room for adjustments during some aspects of the prioritization process. Primarily, the process requires that teachers constantly seek the "multifaceted, complex ideas" and logically connect other skills and concepts to these ideas in order for the benefits of the process to be fully realized, thus making learning more relevant for students.

CLUSTERING STANDARDS

Clustering standards is the process that follows the prioritization process. Prioritizing the standards, as was just detailed, allows us to gain a deeper understanding of the content and skills described by the standards, again so that we can identify the big ideas. Once the big ideas have been identified within the standards, we must then think about how other standards are related to, support, and/or are contextualized within the overarching concept. Standards can relate to one another and be clustered in two ways: (1) within the same content area, or (2) across subjects (interdisciplinary).

Clustering by Content Area

In many cases, for students to conceptually grasp the overarching concepts found within content standards, they are required to have prerequisite knowledge or skills in order to understand and master complex ideas. While this need for a prior knowledge base or skills is often inherent to the standards, the ways in which standards are organized do not always reflect a self-evident and clear conceptual progression of the prerequisite skills and knowledge that is implied by the standard in order for students to grasp the overarching concept. Thus it is important to identify the standards that represent the central focus for a unit, and then identify other standards within the unit that function in support of the central focus. Figure 2.8 demonstrates a set of standards clustered within the same content area in which the P1 standards represent the multifaceted, complex ideas for students to master within this unit, and the P2 standards serve as prerequisite skills or knowledge that conceptually support the P1 standards.

The first thing to notice about this cluster of 5th-grade English/Language Arts standards is that there are three P1 standards that comprise the anchors for this unit. This points out an important fact, that it is quite possible to have more than one P1 standard within the same unit. In this case, it is clear from looking at the first two P1 standards that the overarching focus for this unit will be understanding the elements of effective narratives (stories), both written and spoken. In order to write an effective narrative, students must use multiple skills (e.g., establishing a plot, point of view, setting, and conflict) and understand how these elements work together in order to create an effective narrative.

Therefore, Standard 1 represents a multifaceted, complex idea and will serve as a P1. Standard 2 in this unit is the "speaking" equivalent to Standard 1 and requires the same combination of multiple skills; however, these skills will simply be used and demonstrated in a different format—speaking instead of writing. Often language arts standards incorporate parallel thinking that requires a similar understanding of concepts (in this case the elements of a narrative), yet the standards ask students to demonstrate their understanding of these concepts in different ways (speaking vs. writing). Such parallel standards can be clustered together in order to help maintain consistency in the concepts being taught (e.g., the elements of a narrative) and provide a natural context for students to demonstrate their understanding of these elements in more than one way (speaking vs. writing).

The third P1 standard is conceptually related to the other two P1 standards in that in order to write a narrative story or verbally deliver a narra-

Figure 2.8. English Cluster Example

P1 Standards (anchors for the unit)

1. Write narratives
   —Establish a plot, point of view, setting, and conflicts.
   —Show, rather than tell, the events of the story.

2. Deliver narrative presentations
   —Establish a situation, plot, point of view, and setting with descriptive words and phrases.
   —Show, rather than tell, the listener what happens.

3. Draw inferences, conclusions, or generalizations about text and support them with textual evidence and prior knowledge.

P2 Standards (conceptually support P1 standards)

1. Discern main ideas and concepts presented in text identifying and assessing evidence.

2. Contrast the actions, motives (e.g., loyalty, selfishness, conscientiousness), and appearances of characters in a work of fiction and discuss the importance of the contrasts to the plot or theme.

3. Create multiple-paragraph narrative compositions:
   a. Establish and develop a situation or plot.
   b. Describe the setting.
   c. Present an ending.

4. Read aloud narrative and expository text fluently and accurately and with appropriate pacing, intonation, and expression.

5. Engage the audience with appropriate verbal cues, facial expressions, and gestures.

6. Use a thesaurus to identify alternative word choices and meanings.

7. Use correct capitalization.

---

tive presentation, students need models of how textual evidence provides readers clues that enable the reader to draw generalizations, conclusions, and inferences. By including Standard 3 in this unit, this teacher recognizes the reciprocal nature of the reading and writing processes. For example, in this unit students will not only be making inferences and drawing conclusions and generalizations from their own reading; they will also be reflecting on the types of textual evidence an author uses in order to help readers make such generalizations and draw conclusions and then use these as models for their own written and spoken narrative presentations.

Standard 3 represents a type of critical thinking that could very easily be taught in isolation, without connecting it to any other standards. Clustering this standard with standards related to writing and delivering narratives may not be self-evident, particularly if the standards are treated as a checklist and taught and assessed in isolation. However, the clustering process provides teachers with an opportunity to identify ways in which standards can be meaningfully connected, such as connecting a standard that requires students to make inferences and draw conclusions to a standard that requires a student to write narratives via the reciprocal nature of the reading and writing process. These types of connections between and among standards are enabled through Strategic Design.

With the P1 standards in place, the remaining task in the clustering process is to identify other standards that relate to or support the P1 standards. In the example above, it is quite clear how the P2 standards represent a series of prerequisite skills or thinking that all contribute to the students' ability to write and deliver effective narrative presentations.

As stated in earlier chapters, students should be the primary beneficiaries of strategically designed curriculum. In this example of clustered standards, the benefit to students is the way in which the teacher explicitly connects the discrete skills taught within the P2 standards with the overarching concepts in the P1 standards. Instead of teaching skills in isolation, the teacher is explicitly connecting the use of these skills to the overarching concept from Day 1 of this unit, and communicating these connections to students every day. Often we see students take little interest in a subject because they fail to understand or have never discovered how the prerequisite skills enable more complex (often times more authentic) thinking or the application of such skills. Sports analogies are perfect examples of this concept. No athletes would come to practice if they knew that there would never be an opportunity to use the skills they are developing and honing during practice. We need to present such opportunities to students prior to asking them to simply practice so that they will not only understand why learning isolated skills or pieces of knowledge is important, but so that they will also be more inclined (motivated) to do so.

Interdisciplinary Clustering (Across Subjects)

In some cases, the contextual relationship between standards can be described by similar themes or topics they all contain. We can bring further relevance to the content students are engaged in by identifying thematic patterns that occur within and across subject areas, and then demonstrating these patterns in explicit ways to students. The overarching concept (P1 standard) anchors the unit, and the P2 and P3 standards serve as support to the broader, more complex concepts inherent within the P1 standard (see, for example, Figure 2.9).

Clustering standards thematically across disciplines enables teachers to demonstrate relevance in learning material that is skill-based in nature or requires a fair amount of foundational knowledge that alone may seem irrelevant, but once applied to a unique or seemingly unrelated concept, the value of such skills/foundational knowledge become apparent. For example, in the thematic cluster of standards above, the P2 math standards, when taught in isolation, may not enthuse all students because the relative value of learning such math concepts is not made explicitly apparent to students. However, thematically clustering such math skills with science standards related to motion demonstrates to students how they can use such math skills to help them identify the effect that forces of motion have on the object.

When beginning the work of clustering standards, it is helpful to think of the P1 standard as a large magnet. Picture the magnet in your hand as you move your hand across all the content standards. The standards that are drawn to your magnet, either within the same content area, across content areas, or both, are those that should be clustered together. In most cases, units with multiple standards will be taught over the course of several weeks and broken into smaller lessons. Each time a specific skill or

---

Figure 2.9. Sample Clusters: Thematic Clustering Across Subjects

P1 Standard from Science

- Knows that laws of motion can be used to determine the effects of forces on the motion of objects (e.g., objects change their motion only when a net force is applied; whenever one object exerts force on another, a force equal in magnitude and opposite in direction is exerted on the first object; the magnitude of the change in motion can be calculated using the relationship $F = ma$, which is independent of the nature of the force)

P2 Standards from Math

- Uses expressions, equations, inequalities, and matricies to represent situations that involve variable quantities and translates among these representations

- Uses a variety of models (e.g., written statement, algebraic formula, table of input-output values, graph) to represent functions, patterns, and relationships

- Uses a variety of methods (e.g., with graphs, algebraic methods, and matricies) to solve systems of equations and inequalities

---

piece of knowledge is taught within a lesson, it should be connected to the big idea for students. This can only happen if those connections are made by the teacher, through clustering, in advance of classroom teaching.

It is important to realize that the process used for prioritizing standards is intrinsically tied to our pedagogical strategies itself, as both are processes of discovery and will fundamentally change the way we teach. The prioritization process becomes a way of thinking about standards and ultimately provides educators with a new lens through which to examine standards-based instruction. The thinking accomplished in this stage of the Strategic Design process will serve well throughout Stages Two (assessment) and Three (instruction).

CHAPTER 3

Stage Two:
Aligning Assessments

In the field of education, the word *assessment* carries several connotations, particularly in relation to school accountability. Indeed, given the current turmoil in the field of education, the varied and accrued meanings of assessment circumscribe what can be fairly called a politics of assessment. As the latter part of this chapter will explore, assessment within the Strategic Design model focuses on the use of assessment as a means of determining student progress, guiding classroom instruction, and directing students in their own learning. However, we would be remiss if we did not briefly discuss the larger context within which classroom instruction is evaluated, that being standardized testing.

Annual testing determines the success of schools, and these results are then often used to evaluate the success of the principal and individual teacher effectiveness, and even impacts the reputation of the school district. The bottom line is that standardized testing has become the centerpiece of evaluating the effectiveness of schools—and it does not appear that we will see the disappearance of such accountability measures in the near future.

Given this educational environment, attention must be paid to who the users of assessments are and how the varied forms of assessment are being used. Quite simply, assessments are used by each level of stakeholders in the school system: From students to the national government, any and all groups who play a part in education have an interest in assessments and their outcomes, and not surprisingly, the results are often politically valenced differently by each of the groups. It is important to note that assessment data are rarely pure or neutral. The quantifiable data from assessment activities has both symbolic and cultural capital.

When we look at the national government, standardized assessment measures are used to determine which states have a "good" educational system and which states are "failing" the students they serve. States then use assessments to determine which districts and schools are performing at the expected levels. In both of these instances, assessments are used as a single tool to evaluate effectiveness, an evaluation that is more often than not contextualized politically, and thus surrounded by controversy.

Although the political aspects and realities of assessment may appear to plague school-level educators, it is critical that we learn to negotiate this sometimes treacherous political terrain. To that end, we must begin to think critically about how to live with the politics of assessment while making assessment activities at the school and classroom levels a valuable tool for evaluating individual student performance and informing teaching practice. Thus assessment must be utilized as a tool that positively enables our primary function—educating children. While the political ramifications endemic to assessment activities will continue to infiltrate our classrooms, we must do our best to understand the role of standardized testing while implementing productive assessment methods in which students are provided with the opportunity to demonstrate their knowledge and inform their academic growth. As a matter of practice, both standardized testing and classroom-based assessments must be utilized if we are to improve our educational system. Effective measurement of student progress, brought about by teachers engaged in the work of designing assessments and analyzing data to inform their instruction, can provide a solid foundation upon which we can transform pedagogy in the classroom. And although we can implement a truly inspiring and informative assessment system in our classrooms, we will still be faced with the task of addressing statewide standardized tests.

The good news is that states have finally begun to align their annual testing to content standards. Thus we must take advantage of this current situation and begin to ensure that we are providing high-quality, standards-aligned classroom instruction. This book is built upon the belief that teachers should be instructional designers, and calls upon teachers to do what they do best: create learning environments that support student learning and inspire students to demonstrate success in all types of settings—whether in a daily journal or on a standardized test. By providing classrooms that are based on intelligent instructional design, students can be successful in all arenas of education, and this shift of focus allows us to negotiate the politics that are necessarily implicated in the work we do as educators.

Assessment needs to serve a greater function than that of merely ranking schools, classroom grading, or determining the "success" of teachers and individual students. In their seminal work on student-involved classroom assessment, Chappuis and Stiggins (2002) assert that in order for classrooms to become more responsive to the specific needs of students, we must begin to rethink what assessment is and how and when we use it. Assessment must support student learning and inform classroom instruction, allowing both students and teachers to continuously improve.

UNDERSTANDING A STRATEGIC APPROACH TO ASSESSMENT

Stage Two of the Strategic Design process begins by taking what we are calling a "strategic approach" to assessment. Within the schema of this chapter, the praxis aspects of assessment are broken down into three units: understanding what is involved in taking a strategic approach to assessment, learning how to select assessments that appropriately measure the mastery of skills and knowledge required by the standard, and, finally, ensuring that assessments are aligned to standards. Each of these broader units are further subdivided into their critical components, as will be made clear as the chapter progresses.

While we feel there is no need to summarize or preview what follows in the ensuing sections, it is important to give the reader a sense of our guiding principles in formulating this chapter. First and foremost, we want to foreground the temporal shift that accompanies our views of assessment: It is critical to note that within Strategic Design, the considerations of assessment come *prior* to the identification of instructional strategies. We feel very strongly, that unless the instructional designer—namely, the teacher—has a clear sense of direction, in terms of what the instruction is intended to achieve for the student as learner, the instruction cannot be adequately designed.

Our second guiding principle, which also takes a markedly different path from conventional conceptualizations and practices of assessment, is the degree to which we involve the students. Within orthodox understandings of assessments, the latter comes at the end of instruction, often with an element of "surprise." It is generally thought that this aspect of surprise, as it obtains in assessment, is somehow critical to our testing of the student's knowledge. In our formulation of strategic assessment, however, this element of surprise is scrupulously removed. Students are fully aware of what types of assessment they will engage in, as well as the skills and knowledge that are to be tested by the assessment. Within our conceptualization of strategic assessment, the students become self-directed learners because they are fully aware, prior to instruction, of what it is they are expected to learn. With these two principles in mind, in the remainder of the chapter, we present a step-by-step guide through our process of strategic assessment.

Assumptions of Strategic Assessment

Designing Assessment Prior to Instruction

Teachers design the assessment immediately after prioritizing and clustering the content standards and prior to the design of instructional activities. This temporal shift as to when assessment design occurs in Strategic Design is a critical difference between strategic assessment and traditional assessment design. Designing assessment prior to identifying instructional strategies ensures a much tighter alignment to standards. Quite simply, instructional strategies will be more focused once teachers have already identified how they will assess student mastery of content standards. It is only after teachers know where they want to take students (assessment) that they can accurately and effectively design classroom instruction or choose instructional activities specifically aligned to the assessment.

Recall the example of Ms. Kwon that we presented in Chapter 1. It was only after she redesigned her assessment (the dissection with the constructed responses in which students were required to label the parts of the digestive system and describe their functions) that she was able to rethink her instruction. Once she knew exactly what her assessment parameters were, she was able to plan her instructional strategies with the particular focus of providing students with the knowledge and skills necessary to be successful on the assessment. In this way, assessment served as the guide to designing effective instruction.

Designing assessments prior to instruction and just after prioritizing and clustering standards also ensures that the assessment will be specifically aligned to the standards, and that teachers are actually assessing mastery of all the standards they intend to address in the unit. It is more effective to design assessments immediately after the prioritization and clustering process because the content and analysis that teachers undergo as a result of Stage One of the Strategic Design process is still fresh in a teacher's mind. Sequencing the process in this way ensures an effective assessment without being distracted with the details of planning instruction at the same time. In fact, once the assessment is designed, it becomes easier for teachers to think about the types of instructional activities and resources they will need to effectively teach the unit. When done effectively, this process streamlines the curriculum design process, enabling teachers to develop standards-aligned classrooms.

Presenting Assessment Detail and Grading Criteria to Students

In another critically important move, prior to beginning a lesson or unit, the assessment details and grading criteria are presented to students. This allows students to understand what they are expected to know and be able to do prior to engaging in the content, empowering them to become self-directed learners. Ideally, exemplars are also provided to students at the beginning of the lesson or unit and students are allowed to engage in the examination of the quality of the exemplars in relation to the rubric or grading criteria. Again, this process, although it is time-consuming, provides a concrete representation to the students of what constitutes excellent work, helping them to be more goal-oriented and self-directed in their learning process.

We believe very strongly that assessment should not be a surprise (as it so often is in most classrooms), but rather a process that provides students with the opportunity to be aware up front of the content that the teacher determined was most important, and thus be better prepared to demonstrate mastery of that content. Assessment, as it is conceived and positioned in the Strategic Design process, is a means for students to get an objective and advance look at what they are expected to know and be able to do.

Because of the patterns of teaching and student expectations that prevail, this is the element of the model that teachers seem to struggle with the most. So often we hear, "But isn't that cheating? Why should students know what is on the test before they take it?" Overcoming this belief requires a significant shift in our conceptions about what assessment is and what it is intended to do. The traditional view of assessment is one in which tests are given to figure out if students "got it" and to assign a grade. It takes place after instruction has happened. And while we would agree that one function of assessment is certainly to quantify student learning in some measurable way (the assignment of grades, for example), we believe that assessment should serve an even larger and more productive purpose—enabling students to direct their learning. Furthermore, Strategic Design enables students to approach assessment as part of the learning process, rather than being perceived primarily as a punitive measure or merely an activity to be used to assign a grade.

For example, as one high school student related to us, he attributed his success in a history course to "good mind-reading." The first test was a gamble—he needed to determine if he should take the "dates and places" approach, or be prepared to write about broader conceptual issues. Beyond the unpredictability of the first test, he was guaranteed a certain measure of success on the remaining tests because the first test showed him what his history teacher thought was important, and the information would serve to guide his study for the rest of the year. We relate this story to illustrate that students always want to know "what is important" within the learning dynamics of a classroom. As educators, we must look at his experience and ask ourselves, "Is effective assessment really about training students to read the mind of the teacher?" What if some students take longer to figure out what the teacher thinks is important? Or what if some students never figure out how to predict the teacher's opinions? Rather than sending a message that students simply need to "study harder," effective assessment enables students to learn strategically throughout the unit and "study smarter" as they prepare for the test. Within an effective assessment model, the student knows in direct and explicit ways "what is important" to know. Students are much more successful if they know where they are headed. And if our ultimate goal is student success rather than ensuring that our grading books reflect a bell curve, it is in everyone's best interest to plan assessments strategically and articulate the details of the assessments to students prior to starting instruction.

Student as Beneficiary

As no doubt our comments above suggest, Strategic Design emphasizes that students should be the primary beneficiaries of assessment. Stiggins asserts that beyond understanding what assessment is, our professional commitment should invoke "the need for every one of us to make a personal commitment to supporting students' well-being through the effective use of classroom assessment" (Stiggins, 2001, p. 2). They should be actively engaged in assessment as a process, not a culminating (and punitive) event. Students should understand that assessment is ongoing in nature and intended not only to provide feedback on their progress, but also to shape the instructional practices within the classroom. Assessment should be designed to help teachers and students understand *why* learning occurred, rather than just providing information to the teacher and students as to *what* was or was not learned.

As with much of the Strategic Design process, we encourage communication. In that light, assessment should be an ongoing conversation between us, as teachers, and our students. Students must be an active part of the assessment process, not passive recipients of its results or consequences. Ideally, students are always made aware of the fact that they are being assessed, and the teacher is expected to be transparent about the purpose of assessment—to evaluate student needs and proficiencies and redesign classroom instruction based on those assessment results. When assessment is thought about as something that is ongoing, not just something that happens at the end, it becomes a vehicle through which students can engage in the content. Strategic assessment assists students in determining to what extent they have mastered the content. Effective assessment systems engage students in evaluating their own proficiency, identifying areas of strength and deficiency, and empowers them to dig deep into the content with the confidence that they are headed in the right direction. This way, the student experiences assessment not as a top-down, sometimes punitive measure of learning, but as part of the entire process of learning.

For example, after realizing that students performed poorly on a homework assignment, Ms. Hernandez asked each student to pick one problem they missed and provide a written description of how they solved the problem in their journals. This was not only an opportunity for students to detail how they had solved the problem they initially had difficulties with, but an opportunity for Ms. Hernandez as well to analyze where and how her students struggled. That night, she reviewed each journal and responded with some insight as to why a student may have had difficulties, and with suggestions for improving performance. With this kind of an approach to the assessment process, it did not take long for Ms. Hernandez's students to realize that her first priority was to ensure that her students were being provided with the support necessary to be successful. In her classroom, assessment was not viewed as a means for the teacher to catch students who were "bad at math," but rather an opportunity to engage students in the process of identifying their own mistakes and articulating how they might be more successful. Rather than simply using assessment to assign a grade, teachers must now look at assessment as a means for providing both qualitative and quantitative feedback to students on their academic progress, learning goals, and personal growth.

Strategic Assessment to Inform Instructional Planning

Once the process of rethinking assessment as we have been describing takes hold, teachers come to realize that a critically important aspect of that engagement is the realization that strategic assessment informs instructional planning. One of the key aspects of our model that bears reiteration is that *effective assessment is by nature ongoing*. Therefore, effective assessment should provide ample evidence regarding the extent to which students have or have not mastered content at various intervals or benchmarks, not just at the end of a unit or a year of study. When assessment results demonstrate a lack of mastery at a certain interval, rather than continuing to move forward, teachers should make appropriate adjustments in their instruction in order to allow for more opportunities for students to engage in a topic prior to moving to the next interval. In this way, assessment continuously informs instructional planning by directing and redirecting the teacher's instructional decisions and planning.

Finally, strategic assessment serves as a basis for analysis of instructional effectiveness. If a student performs poorly on an assessment, rather than simply blaming the student for not studying hard enough, as teachers we should examine the instructional activities or learning opportunities provided for that student in relation to the assessment. Perhaps the instructional activities did not give the student the appropriate or ample

opportunity to practice the skills and obtain the content required to perform well on the assessment. In this way, assessment is used to improve
both teacher and student practice.

We are not suggesting that if students perform poorly on a test, either
the teacher or the student is solely at fault. We are simply saying that assessment provides a window into both the student's understanding and
the teacher's instructional design. By looking through this window, we can
begin to identify the causes of student success and failure. These causes
may be attributed to students, or the teacher, or both. Identifying why a
student "got it" or didn't "get it" is complex, and assessment serves as a
way to deconstruct the reasons why students performed well or poorly so
that we can replicate good instruction or fix ineffective instruction.

Having understood the concept and reasons behind the need to approach the process of assessment differently, now we must make yet
another shift in our pedagogical practices to transition into becoming
Strategic Designers of assessment. This practice challenges teachers to
think specifically about the *continuous* aspect of the assessment process
that we have been advocating.

STRATEGIC ASSESSMENT:
SELECTING ASSESSMENTS TO MEASURE STANDARD MASTERY

Considerations for Successful Assessment Design

Effectively assessing student mastery of content standards is challenging
work. In order to ensure that the assessment measures what it is intended
to, teachers must be extremely thoughtful about assessment design. To assist with the assessment design process, Strategic Design asks teachers to
consider the following questions:

1. What assessment methods are available?
2. What are the advantages and disadvantages of the methods?
3. How well does the assessment align to the standard(s) being
    assessed?

Available Assessment Methods

The first consideration for teachers when engaging in the assessment
design process is to determine what methods are available for use. Within
the Strategic Design model, four types of assessment methods are utilized:
selected response assessment, constructed response assessment, performance assessment, and personal communication. In our experience,

every assessment available for use falls into one of these four categories. The key to good assessment design, however, is in understanding that the most effective classroom assessment system will likely employ a variety of methods. Nor do these multiple assessment methods have to operate independently of one another. For example, a math teacher may design an assessment in which students are asked to select the most appropriate answer from a given list of choices and then describe their rationale—this would be a hybrid of the selected response and constructed response assessments methods. We do not privilege one method over another; our primary concern is in discerning which assessment method is most appropriate for a given learning outcome. In fact, we believe that there is a time and a place for every type of assessment. We are most interested in determining which method will most effectively assess student mastery of the standard. In order to do this, we must consider the advantages and disadvantages of each assessment method.

Advantages and Disadvantages of Each Method

Not surprisingly, there are advantages and disadvantages inherent to any assessment method that may be chosen. Therefore, as teachers and assessors, we must look critically at the benefits and drawbacks of each of the four assessment methods in an effort to determine when each (or combinations thereof) would be the most effective choice. An unbiased examination of the benefits and drawbacks of each method will assist teachers in determining the circumstances in which one assessment method may be preferable over another.

The intent of this chapter is not to provide a predetermined formula that can then be utilized to yield "the best" type of assessment overall; the complex dynamics of specific student learning situations would preclude such an attempt. Sometimes the most complex assessments are also the most appropriate, and sometimes they are overburdensome. Likewise, a relatively simple assessment can provide the needed information, or fall short of truly measuring student mastery of standards. Ultimately, the teacher's task is to make informed and strategic decisions about what types of assessments offer the best in terms of both efficiency and effectiveness for a given set of standards. A detailed consideration for making these determinations, as well as additional tools to aid the process, are shared later in this chapter.

Alignment of the Assessment to the Standard(s) Being Assessed

The final consideration for assessment design is how well it aligns to the standard(s) being assessed. Specifically, the cognition requirements in Bloom's taxonomy should be considered when designing an aligned assessment. And while cognition requirements may, upon first glance, appear to be too complex to assess, with the right framework this process opens up countless possibilities for effective and efficient classroom assessments. As described in Chapter 2, as teachers prioritize standards, they must consider the level of Bloom's taxonomy required by the standard. Likewise, when designing assessments, we need to identify the level of cognition in Bloom's that can be assessed by a given assessment method.

As we have elaborated previously, in Strategic Design, Bloom's taxonomy is the critical link between prioritized standards and assessment methods. Our assertion is that assessment is effective only if the assessment method accurately measures the level of thinking required by the standard. Assessments are not valid when there are mismatches between the method used to assess and the desired level of achievement. For example, although one could assess that students knew the name of the President by having them write an essay, it would be much more efficient to have them complete a fill-in-the-blank or multiple-choice question to assess this knowledge. In other words, teachers must ensure that they are not employing overly burdensome assessment methods just for the sake of utilizing a specific method. Conversely, a multiple-choice assessment may not be sufficient to measure a student's reasoning ability, and so a more open-ended method would be warranted. We will explore this concept in greater detail below.

The remainder of this chapter is dedicated to accomplishing two objectives: 1) to provide a common definition of each of the four assessment methods and evaluate their advantages and disadvantages, and 2) to assist the reader in developing a process for identifying the most effective and efficient assessment method for a given set of learning outcomes or standards.

THE FOUR ASSESSMENT METHODS: ADVANTAGES AND DISADVANTAGES

An extensive amount of theory and research is available on classroom-based assessment methods. For our purposes, after consulting the field of available literature, we have privileged the work of Richard Stiggins in defining assessment methods. In addition to defining and exploring each assessment method, we will evaluate the advantages and disadvantages of each, including the ability of each method to assess the different levels of cognition as defined by Bloom's taxonomy. While the tables in the text below provide a thorough and summative look at the advantages and disadvantages of each method, this list is by no means exhaustive. Our intent in this chapter is to highlight the fact that teachers should be critical evaluators of assessment methods and be strategic about which method provides the most effective and efficient means of measuring the intended student achievement. As we discuss later in this chapter, a careful evaluation of each of the assessment methods will greatly contribute to efficacy of the overall process of aligning assessments to standards.

Selected Response Assessment

Selected response assessment is the method that most educators are familiar with, particularly in an era of standardized testing. Selected response tests are often in a paper-and-pencil format that requires students to select an answer from a set of possible solutions. This method typically has a distinct "right" answer, and is lauded as a more objective approach to assessment. Examples of selected response assessments are: multiple-choice, true/false, fill-in-the-blank, matching, and short-answer–type responses.

Figures 3.1 and 3.2 provide a snapshot of the advantages and disadvantages of selected response assessment, as well as the levels of Bloom's most appropriately assessed by this method.

This assessment method is most effective at measuring knowledge and comprehension (Bloom's Levels I and II). By contrast, it is difficult to capture a student's reasoning ability using such a restrictive format. A correct answer on a selected response assessment will only tell the teacher that the student applied correct reasoning or recalled the requested

FIGURE 3.1. Selected Response Assessment: Pros and Cons

Pros	Cons
Easy to score	Narrows student's ability to demonstrate knowledge
Objective	
Easy to administer and grade	Difficult to construct
Quick	Appeals to limited learning styles
Straightforward for students	Difficult to assess beyond basic knowledge and facts. Students can guess and get the right answer— may not be measuring student knowledge.
Good practice for the mandated standardized exams	
Easy to collect data from results	

Figure 3.2. Sample Standards for Selected Response Assessments

LEVELS OF BLOOM'S
Knowledge
Comprehension

Know waves carry energy from one place to another.

Identify idioms, analogies, metaphors, and similes in prose and poetry.

Locate on maps of North and South America land claimed by Spain, France, England, Portugal, the Netherlands, Sweden, and Russia.

Know the definition of *conditional probability.*

Know Earth is composed of several layers: a cold, brittle lithosphere; a hot, convecting mantle; and a dense, metallic core.

Find the area of a rectangle.

---

information (or guessed well) or did not. However, it is hard for a teacher to discern *why* a student answered a question correctly or incorrectly without further information. Therefore, selected response is good for measuring basic recall of facts of knowledge but is not the best option when trying to identify exactly where a student's thinking is strong and where it is deficient. Figure 3.2 provides sample standards that demonstrate the level of cognition that is most effectively measured by selected response assessment.

Again, one should remember that we are only providing a guide for the conversation. Ultimately, it is you, the teacher, who should decide if the method is appropriate for the level of Bloom's.

Constructed Response Assessment

Constructed response assessments call for an extended written answer. Students are asked to respond to a question, provide an explanation for a response, or analyze a topic and discuss their analysis. Typically, the response is scored by the teacher using a rubric or against a set of grading criteria. While this assessment method is often thought of in terms of the content related to English/Language Arts (e.g., writing essays), this method can be applied across content areas.

For example, students might detail scientific reasoning or explain their answer to an open-ended math problem. Examples of constructed response assessments include: writing an essay to a specific prompt, written interpretation of scientific information, solving problems and explaining reasoning.

We have provided Figure 3.3 as a snapshot of the advantages and disadvantages of constructed response assessment.

FIGURE 3.3. Constructed Response Assessment: Pros and Cons

Pros	Cons
Provides deeper window into student's thinking	Time-consuming to complete and grade
Can determine exactly where a student's reasoning is strong and where it is weak	Difficult for English Language Learners to demonstrate their understanding due to language barrier
Allows teacher to provide more specific feedback to student	Grading is more subjective

This is a relatively flexible assessment method that can be used to measure several levels of cognition. Because responses are often open-ended, it can be useful for evaluating as much or as little student knowledge as is required. Additionally, within this method the teacher is able to design questions aimed at eliciting specific feedback from students, be it comprehension or evaluation. That being said, this method, when designed carefully and thoughtfully, can be used to evaluate Levels II through VI of Bloom's taxonomy. Figure 3.4 provides examples of the kinds of standards that might best be measured using a constructed response assessment.

FIGURE 3.4. Sample Standards for Constructed Response Assessments

LEVELS OF BLOOM'S
Comprehension
Application
Analysis
Synthesis
Evaluation

Describe temperature and heat flow in terms of the motion of molecules (or atoms).

Use properties of numbers to demonstrate whether assertions are true or false.

Explain the influence and achievements of significant leaders of the time (e.g., John Marshall, Andrew Jackson, Chief Tecumseh, Chief Logan, Chief John Ross, Sequoyah).

Compare and contrast the presentation of a similar theme or topic across genres to explain how the selection of genre shapes the theme or topic.

Explain the early democratic ideas and practices that emerged during the colonial period, including the significance of representative assemblies and town meetings.

Use a variety of methods, such as words, numbers, symbols, charts, graphs, tables, diagrams, and models, to explain mathematical reasoning.

Use properties of numbers to construct simple, valid arguments (direct and indirect) for, or formulate counterexamples to, claimed assertions.

Performance Assessment

In a performance assessment, a student performs an observable activity allowing the teacher to evaluate the student's process or product. It is critical that teachers understand that students can be assessed both through observable processes and through completed products. This method of assessment is often referred to as an "authentic" assessment method because of its ability to simulate real-life experiences. This is the case when assessing an observable process, such as speaking a foreign language or playing an instrument. However, it is also quite possible, and useful, to assess a product that resulted from the performance. The product can be assessed independently of the performer. A science fair exhibit is a good example of a performance assessment that can be assessed independently from the performer. Therefore, in designing this type of assessment, teachers must determine if they are grading the process, the product, or both.

Examples of performance assessments include speaking a foreign language, making a speech, a dramatic performance, a science lab or project, reading aloud, term papers and research reports.

The primary advantages of a performance assessment are the versatility and depth of information it offers to teachers. However, the trade-off for that depth is in the complexity of, and time spent in, implementing such performance assessments (see Figure 3.5). They often require extensive preparation, such as rubrics, lengthy assignment descriptions, and multiple materials. They can also be time-consuming to grade and are more prone to teacher subjectivity.

While performance assessments could be used to assess any level of cognition, they are too time-consuming and complex if the teacher only wants to measure knowledge or comprehension. This method is clearly the best way to evaluate a student's *application* of knowledge and comprehension. Performance assessments also are very helpful in assessing high levels of

FIGURE 3.5. Performance Assessment: Pros and Cons

Pros	Cons
Mirrors authentic tasks	Time-consuming
Engaging	Difficult to grade
Provides for wide range of learning styles	Can be subjective
Allows students to express creativity	
Can assess both *process* of completing a task as well as the final *product*	

cognition such as synthesis or analysis. Figure 3.6 demonstrates some of the standards performance assessments are best suited to measure.

FIGURE 3.6. Sample Standards for Performance Assessments

LEVELS OF BLOOM'S
Application
Analysis
Synthesis
Evaluation

Use speaking techniques, including voice modulation, inflection, tempo, enunciation, and eye contact, for effective presentations.

Know how to build a simple compass and use it to detect magnetic effects, including Earth's magnetic field.

Decode two-syllable nonsense words and regular multisyllable words.

Measure the length of an object to the nearest inch and/or centimeter.

Write a friendly letter complete with the date, salutation, body, closing, and signature.

Construct a cube and rectangular box from two-dimensional patterns and use these patterns to compute the surface area for these objects.

Personal Communication

Personal communication is the assessment method, in our experience, that is the most underutilized. Personal communication is communicating with students verbally for the sake of assessing knowledge. Teachers spend much of their time talking to students. We have found, however, that it is often informal in nature and rarely thought of, and thus effectively utilized, as a means of assessing what a student knows. Therefore, we bring this to your attention with the hopes of encouraging skillful dialogue and strategic questioning. For example, when talking with students, teachers should have a clear goal in mind. Is the goal to simply ask clarifying questions that can be answered with a simple yes or no? Or is the intent of the communication to probe deeper into a student's thinking? Depending on the teacher's purpose, the types of questions asked of the student should vary and be intentional. A clarifying request might be as simple as asking a student to restate something, while communication intended to probe deeper into a student's thinking will likely be more open-ended. Once again, there is an appropriate use for each of these types of communications in the classroom. The key to effective personal communication is to be intentional in how we communicate and with what purpose in order to facilitate the intended response.

Personal communication is one of the most flexible means of assessment—it provides very specific and useful information to the teacher regarding a student's thoughts, opinions, or knowledge. Examples of personal communication assessments include Socratic questioning, conferences, interviews, class discussions, talking to students on the playground.

While it may not be used to its fullest potential, there are some distinct advantages to thinking about personal communication as a means to assess students, the greatest of those being the relationships built between the teacher and student. The most obvious disadvantages are how much time it takes and how hard it is to record (see Figure 3.7). That being said, it is conceivable that a teacher might record interviews with students and evaluate the responses. However, as former classroom teachers, we acknowledge that the time and effort involved in this method are extremely prohibitive.

Personal communication can be used to evaluate virtually any level of cognition. However, there is an additional intent when using personal communication, such as individualizing instruction, building relationships, or developing student communication skills. Teachers should carefully weigh the costs and the benefits of using this method, and develop clarity about the purpose of using personal communication rather than one of the other three methods. It is important to note that this assessment method is particularly useful for individual students who are struggling on a particular concept or in general. Although the teacher may determine that this assessment method is not particularly efficient to accomplish the intended objective, it is likely to be the perfect means of assessing the progress of an individual or small group of students. Figure 3.8 presents examples of the kinds of standards that are an especially good fit for a personal communication assessment.

Now that you have an understanding of the four assessment methods that are available, the critical work is to determine which method serves as the most effective and efficient way to assess your learning objectives.

Figure 3.7. Personal Communication Assessment: Pros and Cons

Pros	Cons
Can be used at a moment's notice	Time-consuming
Can probe more deeply through questioning	Hard to record responses/ grades
Can easily involve parents in the process, through conferences	Subjective
Helps build relationships between teacher and student	Relies on relationships between teacher and student

FIGURE 3.8. Sample Standards for Personal Communication Assessments

LEVELS OF BLOOM'S
Knowledge
Comprehension
Application
Analysis
Synthesis
Evaluation

Respond to persuasive messages with questions, challenges, or affirmations.

Ask and answer simple questions related to data representations.

Describe the properties of common objects and communicate observations orally.

Pose relevant questions about events they encounter in historical documents, eyewitness accounts, oral histories, letters, diaries, artifacts, photographs, maps, artworks, and architecture.

REQUIREMENTS OF ASSESSMENT

In Strategic Design, we use two criteria to aid in the alignment of assessments to standards: 1) cognitive requirements of standards and assessments, and 2) implementation requirements of the assessment. Each of these criteria is described in more detail below. It is critical that instructional designers develop an "efficiency/effectiveness quotient" that can guide their thinking about which assessments are the best match for a given standard or set of standards. This process can be used to evaluate the alignment of existing assessments, or to develop new assessments.

Criterion 1: Cognitive Requirements

As described previously, Bloom's taxonomy has been our guiding framework for determining the level of cognition required by a standard or an assessment. The essential question here is: *"What type of assessment will require students to perform the level that is required by the standard?"* For example, if a standard requires students to "interpret data" (Bloom's Level IV—analysis), then the assessment should also require them to interact with data on an analytical level. Thus the primary step in determining the alignment of an assessment is to determine whether it engages students in activities that are at the appropriate cognitive level as required by the standard(s).

We have developed Figure 3.9 to assist in the alignment of Bloom's taxonomy to the various assessment methods. And while we have attempted

Figure 3.9. Bloom's Taxonomy Assessment Alignment Chart

Level of Bloom's	Selected Response	Constructed Response	Performance Assessment	Personal Communication
I Knowledge	This is an efficient and objective way to quickly gauge student knowledge of discreet facts.	You can get at knowledge with this method, but it may be inefficient, or somewhat subjective.	Not recommended— too inefficient.	
II Comprehension	Well-crafted questions can measure students' comprehension, but will not get at their actual reasoning.	This is an efficient and effective way to measure comprehension, and determine the nuances of student understanding.	Not recommended— too inefficient.	
III Application	Not recommended—does not demonstrate ability to apply knowledge and comprehension.	This type of assessment can only measure applications in the written form.	Students can demonstrate written, oral, and physical applications of knowledge and understanding.	This can be both an effective and efficient way to measure any level of Bloom's, but may be hard to formally record or track.
IV Analysis	Not recommended—does not effectively provide evidence of desired analytical thinking.	Students can construct responses that clearly indicate their analytical process.	The teacher would have to measure *both* process and product to truly get at students' analytical thinking.	
V Synthesis	Not recommended—does not effectively provide evidence of desired synthesis processes.	Students can construct responses that clearly describe their process of synthesizing information.	Students can demonstrate their ability to compile and reformulate information in a number of different ways.	
VI Evaluation	Not recommended—does not effectively provide evidence of desired evaluative thinking.	Students can construct responses that clearly demonstrate their evaluative capabilities.	Students can present and defend their judgments and opinions in an interactive setting that delves deeply into their thinking.	

Note: Shading indicates a strong match.

to provide a fairly comprehensive and utilitarian list of appropriate assessment matches, it is critical to remember that this is not an exact science. Once again, the most important aspect of this process is the freedom it provides teachers to think critically about how to most effectively identify and design the best assessment for the standard being addressed.

Criterion 2: Implementation Requirements

Implementation requirements refer to the logistical considerations (and constraints) of a given assessment method. Some assessment methods are easy and quick to administer and grade (e.g., true/false test), while others involve considerably more time and planning (e.g., a science lab). The essential question here is: "Is the complexity or time required to implement the assessment justified by the quality of information it will yield?"

There is no way to clearly rank the implementation requirements of each assessment method. A well-crafted multiple-choice test can take a long time to design, whereas a classroom debate (performance assessment) may require a lot of the student's time and only minimal preparation on the teacher's part. The opposite can be true as well. For any type of assessment method, the following considerations can help to ascertain the implementation requirements:

- How much time will it take to design?
- How much time will it take to evaluate?
- How difficult will it be to evaluate? (And how susceptible is it to subjectivity?)
- What kinds of resources will be required to design, implement, and evaluate the assessment?
- Will it produce quantity of data, quality of data, or both?

By evaluating the assessment according to these areas of concern, teachers can make informed decisions about whether the data generated warrant the work it will take to design and implement the assessment.

By taking into account the cognitive and implementation requirements of any given assessment, educators can accurately determine how well the assessment aligns to the relevant standards. While this process may initially appear to be cumbersome, with practice and regular use, like prioritizing and clustering standards, it will become internalized by the user. In this way, strategic analysis of assessment options will become a routine practice for the instructional designer. In the case of assessment design, when assessments are aligned to standards, and teachers and students clearly understand what is expected of them, the net result is increased student achievement.

CHAPTER 4

Stage Three:
Strategic Classroom Instruction

As we have stated throughout the book, Strategic Design for Student Achievement is not a prescriptive model for classroom instruction. It is by no means our aim to provide educators with a set curriculum for use in classrooms across the nation. Rather, it is our goal to challenge teachers to rethink instructional design in order to ensure that it is effective. That being said, this chapter is also not about compiling a list of the "best instructional strategies" available. We do not feel that providing lists and descriptions of strategies is particularly helpful, since countless individuals and organizations have made information of this type readily available.

Given our approach in the previous chapters, it will come as no surprise that what we hope to inspire is an understanding that *instructional strategies are only as effective as the process used to select them.* In other words, even the best strategies will be ineffective if they are not selected according to the intended learning outcomes and implemented with a specific purpose in mind. This chapter will focus on the process of selecting instructional strategies that are sure to assist students in acquiring specific knowledge and meeting the objectives set forth in the first two stages of the Strategic Design process.

THE NATURE OF INSTRUCTION

Teacher as Facilitator

Our entire view of classroom instruction is founded upon the concept of the teacher as facilitator. As educators, we must challenge the traditional conception of teaching in which we are defined and positioned as "instructors." This single word implies a one-way process of teaching, namely that of a teacher who tells students what they need to know or tells them what information to access to find out what they need to know. In order to transform classroom practice and improve learning opportunities for all children, we must rethink our role as instructor and explore what it means to facilitate the acquisition of knowledge. Effective instruction requires that we are responsible for facilitating learning, not simply imparting knowledge. What we mean by this is that a teacher's primary responsibility is to design classroom instruction with the goal of facilitating learning in a manner that most effectively allows students to access and explore the content.

As the research suggests, human beings learn most effectively from interaction and exploration. And although many of us are aware that students must be engaged in their own learning, classroom instruction often fails to acknowledge this fact, and correspondingly we fail to design instruction based on the implications of what that means. We are not suggesting that one should never engage in direct instruction. In fact, the use of direct instruction is a necessary part of effective classroom instruction. However, we are suggesting that direct instruction be used as only one of several methods of engaging students in the content. Perceiving ourselves as facilitators allows teachers to think differently about how to most effectively assist students in their own learning. Even the act of "instructing" will take on new meaning when approached in this way.

As *facilitate* means to make easier or to help bring about, similarly, effective classroom instruction should be designed to enable learning for all students. An effective classroom will employ direct instruction, guided practice, independent exploration, group work, and countless other approaches to learning. Our aim is not to find a strategy that fits all teaching situations, but rather to find the best strategy for achieving the specific objectives for the stated lesson. As the remainder of this chapter makes clear, effective instructional strategies are those that are identified and implemented using a process of informed decisionmaking.

The Definition of "Instruction"

Having already discussed the importance of approaching teaching as a facilitator rather than an instructor, it is important that when we address the third stage of the Strategic Design process—instruction—we define and contextualize our specific usage of the term. At the outset, we want to allay any confusion that may arise from the fact that we maintain the term *instruction*, while we advocate a revisionist approach to *instructor*.

Instruction, as it has been used in the field of education, is a fairly liminal term and has many different connotations. In fact, historically the definition of instruction has changed numerous times to account for the various shifts in pedagogical approaches and theories that have impacted the field in this country in the last hundred years. At its simplest, the term *instruction* is synonymous with strategies for teaching the subject at hand. More often than not, this strategy has manifested itself as the classroom "lecture." Within the presumptions and parameters of this format, the instructor is assumed to have knowledge and expertise about the subject and can ostensibly tell the students everything they need to know. In a traditional and historic sense, the content and delivery of the lecture came to be synonymous with instruction. While lecturing continues to have its place as a form of instruction, it has become widely accepted that lecturing alone is neither the only instructional strategy available, nor is it the most effective option in many cases. Therefore, the educational community has been exploring other means besides lecturing to deliver content. Strategies such as interactive notebooks, graphic organizers, learning centers, and project-based learning, to name just a few, have become widely accepted and are used as alternatives to lecturing. As is the case with many other changes that have played out in the field of education, the pendulum swung completely away from lecturing and toward hands-on activities when the research revealed that straight lecturing was an ineffective way to deliver content to students.

Within the context of Strategic Design, we define instruction as engaging students in the acquisition of knowledge and skills. Classroom instruction is about enabling students to acquire the knowledge they need. When we first started writing this book, we were bound and determined to compartmentalize instructional strategies into an easy-to-understand graphic organizer. We were confident that we could provide educators with a tool that told them exactly what instructional strategy to use based on the cognitive levels they were trying to address. After grappling with this issue for years, and innumerable conversations with colleagues, we have determined that this is an impossible feat. Classroom instruction, in particular good classroom instruction, is a dynamic, complex, ever-evolving process. The number of possible strategies, when combined with the ways in which each strategy may be implemented, provides teachers with literally thousands of ways to deliver content to students. This is both exciting and overwhelming. Thus it was impossible to provide teachers with a *single* way of delivering classroom instruction when faced with such a diversity and range of potential options. Good teaching is about situationally specific thoughtful design.

In our experience, both as teachers and in working as consultants with teachers across the country, instructional "activities" abound. There is certainly no shortage of resources that present a variety of things "to do" in the classroom. Textbooks are packed with such ideas, and anyone who has used the Internet for planning knows that a few key words entered in

Google will yield thousands of ready-made lesson plans, full of activities aimed at engaging students in the content. However, it is critical to note that within Strategic Design, an "activity" or something "to do," without an intended purpose, does not qualify as instruction. Thus the processes that comprise Strategic Design act as a filter for all of these activities, providing a way for teachers to discern which activity has a high likelihood of being effective for their intended purpose.

Instruction is not, in this context, a series of activities that may relate to the unit topic but are not necessarily aligned to standards and assessments. As teachers move from random acts of instruction to strategic instructional decisions, they must determine what, in their arsenal of curriculum and instructional activities, will offer students meaningful opportunities to acquire and practice the knowledge, understanding, and skills required by the standards. Indeed, teachers are often adept at collecting substantial banks of instructional activities. Many are, by nature, excellent activity planners. Furthermore, many teachers are offered predeveloped instructional activities in the form of textbooks and other prepackaged curricula. In many schools and districts, particularly those serving the most underresourced areas, teachers are required to use textbooks and other materials that were adopted at the state level, without any input from teachers in that particular school or district. The message that is delivered with these curricular programs is that they are standards-aligned, and that by following the program with fidelity, teachers will be effectively teaching to, and assessing, all of the required standards.

While these comprehensive curricula can certainly be useful resources that are standards-aligned, most of them are developed for a national audience and are then supplemented or partially modified to meet specific state standards. As a result, many of these programs cover some standards effectively while leaving substantial gaps or weaknesses in other curricular areas. Furthermore, teachers are not guaranteed that the curriculum-embedded assessments are at an appropriate level of rigor to truly meet the standards for their state.

Given the abundance of instructional choices available to teachers, and the inherent gaps between standards and many textbook-based curricula, it is incumbent upon each teacher to make strategic determinations about what to teach, what not to teach, and how to modify their materials to make them align to standards and assessments. In the remainder of this chapter, we present considerations teachers can use to make such determinations and to ensure that everything students do in the classroom is moving them toward mastery of the standards.

Within the Strategic Design model, the third stage of this process is more about thoughtful identification and implementation of strategies than providing teachers with a single strategy to meet a predetermined objective. The bottom line is that there is no one best single option for engaging students in the acquisition of knowledge. There are only good teachers who understand how to effectively identify and implement strategies aimed at engaging students in learning. Even the "best," research-based, differentiated strategy that employs multiple modes of learning can be completely ineffective if not purposefully designed and well-implemented.

Current Research on Effective Instruction

We would be remiss if we did not discuss, at least briefly, the importance of understanding what the research tells us about good instruction. And while we do not purport that every strategy used in the classroom must have a body of research to demonstrate its effectiveness, we do think it is critically important that professionals in the field of education be aware of the body of evidence that provides us with insights into the elements of highly effective classroom instructional strategies. Professional learning communities should provide individual teachers with information about what the research says about specific instructional strategies.

While the body of research on effective instructional practice is voluminous, there are a few researchers whose work particularly complements the Strategic Design process. Specifically, the quality of their research base, their accessibility to teachers, and their utility in practice have proven helpful in their application to Strategic Design. The work of Marzano, Pickering, and Pollock (2001) provided us with guides to the identification of effective instructional strategies that can be used in almost any classroom. Their research and subsequent theories are based on the premise (which is supported by substantial scholarship in the field) that individual teachers can have a significant effect on student achievement. Marzano et al. set out to determine which instructional strategies have a statistically high probability of enhancing student achievement for all students, in all subjects, at all grade levels. The nine strategies they have identified are:

1. identifying similarities and differences
2. summarizing and note-taking
3. reinforcing effort and providing recognition
4. homework and practice
5. nonlinguistic representations
6. cooperative learning
7. setting objectives and providing feedback
8. generating and testing hypotheses
9. cues, questions, and advanced organizers

Although we will not explore these strategies in detail, we highlight them to provide a sense of how the research might be used to help guide one's initial thinking about the identification of strategies to be used in the classroom. Again, our intention is not to suggest that teachers must investigate the research base of each instructional strategy they have used. Rather, teachers should become familiar with the research surrounding effective instructional strategies to use as a starting point when identifying potentially effective classroom strategies. Knowing what is available and understanding how it can be used effectively, as proven by research, will provide the teacher with several options for classroom instruction.

STRATEGIC INSTRUCTION

In Chapter 3 we described the process of aligning assessments to standards and choosing the most efficient and effective assessment method. This work began in Stage Two with a focus on designing a summative assessment that is aligned to the P1 standard(s). In Stage Two we were still focused on the overall unit design and trying to determine the best way to credibly assess the unit as a whole via the summative assessment. Once the summative assessment has been designed, it is time to consider how to move students incrementally toward success on the summative assessment. In other words, how can a teacher break down all the knowledge and skills that the summative assessment will require of students and begin to teach, and assess, each of these elements in smaller, more manageable chunks? These smaller chunks of learning outcomes are often found in the P2 and P3 standards. However, in some cases the P1 standard may need to be broken down into smaller learning outcomes as well.

Having gone through Stages One and Two of the Strategic Design process allows us to have a clear idea of what it is students will have to learn with regard to a specific standard and/or unit. Through the assessment process outlined in the last chapter, teachers are able to determine an appropriate format for assessing student progress toward standard mastery. At this stage of the Strategic Design process it is also important to think about how we inform our instructional effectiveness throughout the unit, before we get to the summative assessment. This occurs through formative assessments.

It is important to remember that formative assessments serve as checkpoints of student proficiency along the way to the summative assessment. Formative assessments assess student proficiency of discrete pieces of knowledge or isolated skills that will be combined in some way to reach proficiency of the summative assessment. It is important to be able to provide feedback to students in relation to the smaller chunks of learning they have to master along the way to accomplishing the larger goals of the unit. This will enable students to have time to make adjustments and/or develop their skills more fully before being asked to combine these discrete skills or isolated facts in a unique way in order to perform well on the summative assessment. The same criteria for choosing the most effective and efficient summative assessment applies to formative assessments as well. At this stage of the Strategic Design process we are drilling down from the big picture unit into daily lessons that comprise that unit. Just as we ask teachers to think about how to assess the unit as a whole via summative assessments, we now want teachers to consider how they will assess instruction incrementally, often daily, throughout the unit. This is formative assessment. One of the best ways to develop formative assessments is to develop measurable learning objectives for the daily lesson. Following is a guiding question and set of guidelines that will help in the development of daily objectives.

> What are the specific, measurable objectives of each lesson that will incrementally move my students toward mastery of the standards (create SMART objectives)?

Creating SMART Objectives

The acronym SMART stands for Specific, Measurable, Aligned to standards, Relevant, and Time-bound.

Specific

Objectives should be specific in that they need to describe precisely what is expected of students. For example, the objective "students will be able to read grade-level text" is too broad. Is the objective referring to decoding skills? Is it referring to fluency rate? Is it referring to comprehension? Based on the way the objective above is written, we cannot discern precisely what students will be expected to do during this lesson, which means, among other consequences, that students will not be able to direct their own learning toward the intended specific learning outcome(s). However, if we were to rewrite the objective as "Students will connect the story being read in class to their personal lives, to another book, and to a historical or current event," we would be able to identify that the focus for this lesson is on making connections in order to build comprehension. Specificity within the objective helps the teacher to more tightly focus the learning for that particular lesson as well as enabling the students to more clearly focus on the expectations for the lesson.

Measurable

Objectives should also be measurable. How will the teacher know that students have accomplished the intended learning for the objective? In the example provided above, one question that students may ask is, "How many connections should we make?" This is a valid question. The expectations outlined in objectives should be quantifiable so that students know precisely what is expected of them. Consequently, the example would be stronger if it described precisely how many connections students should make: "Students will make at least 4 connections between the story being read in class and their personal lives, another book, and a historical or current event."

Aligned to Standards

Objectives should also be aligned to standards. One might think that since objectives are being derived from standards, the alignment between them would be a given; in our experience, this alignment does not happen so naturally. It is critically important for teachers to pay close attention to the language used within objectives to ensure that the objectives require the same level of cognition as the standard. It is also important to note that there may not be a one-to-one correspondence between an objective and a standard. For example, a teacher may determine and identify three objectives that are required to incrementally advance students toward the proficiency inscribed by a single standard; this is perfectly acceptable. In fact, one of the greatest benefits of breaking down standards into discrete objectives is that such a process brings clarity toward fully understanding the standard, as well as the recognition that it is perfectly acceptable to address a standard through smaller, doable components rather than a whole. The following example demonstrates how one standard can be broken down into multiple objectives.

Standard. Students relate current events to the physical and human characteristics of places and regions.

Assessment. Students will produce a written report (to be presented orally) that compares a historical and a present-day natural disaster (e.g., the eruption of Mt St. Helens, the 1906 San Francisco earthquake, the 1989 earthquake, etc.). The report will incorporate the following components:

- An analysis of the physical and human characteristics of the places affected, and how those characteristics impacted the outcomes of the events.

- A description of the changes that occurred between the first and second disaster.
- How the events impacted physical and human characteristics of impacted locations.
- Before-and-after cartographic depiction of the areas impacted by the disaster.

Extra credit may be obtained by comparing an American and a global disaster.

Objectives. By the end of the lesson:

- Students will be able to identify at least 3 physical and 3 human characteristics of the hurricane-damaged areas of Florida.
- Students will be able to create a causal flow chart or other depiction of the hurricane and the damage it created.
- Students will be able to predict how the hurricane's impact would have been different given at least one significant change to the human and/or physical characteristics of the impacted regions (e.g., Florida is raised above sea level or Florida is less densely populated).

In the example provided above, the level of cognition described by the objectives becomes progressively harder. First, students have to *identify* physical and human characteristics of a region. Next, students are asked to create a *cause-and-effect* chart. Finally, students are asked to *predict* how the impact of a current event (in this case the hurricane) would have been different given a change in physical or human characteristics of the region. Clearly there is an incremental progression in the level of cognition required (e.g., moving from identification of characteristics to making a prediction based on a change in one or more of the characteristics). It is also clear to see that when taken together, these objectives are aligned to the standard. However, if only the first objective were listed for the given standard, there would not be sufficient alignment between the standard and the objective. Identifying physical and human characteristics of a region accounts for only part of the standard but does not require students to relate current events to the characteristics of the region.

One way to ensure that the objectives are fully aligned to the standard is to pay close attention to the language used to write objectives. Specifically, the verbs in the objectives that describe what students will be doing should clearly articulate the progression of cognition and/or skill-building that ultimately reaches the level of cognition or skill required by the standard. Once again, we reference Bloom's taxonomy and the key words that accompany each level of the taxonomy. In following the SMART paradigm for writing objectives, we advocate that teachers use the key words (often verbs) from the Bloom's resource (provided in Chapter 2, Figure 2.5) to help them craft their objectives to ensure an alignment between the objectives and the standards.

Relevant

Of course, objectives should be *relevant* to the overall unit; however, it is equally important that these objectives be communicated in ways that make them relevant to students. Thus when developing objectives, teachers should also be thinking about how the objectives will be articulated to students. Certainly, there is value in simply posting the daily objectives on the board; however, there is even more value in having a conversation with students about how the daily objectives are linked to the overall unit. In other words, at the end of the lesson, students should be able to articulate how a particular lesson is relationally positioned to the overall unit. To illustrate, let's look again at the sample objective given earlier regarding reading comprehension. If the objective for the lesson was that "Students will connect the story being read in class to their personal lives, to another book, and to a historical or current event," it would be important to have a conversation with students about how making such connections will enable them to remember and analyze what they read more clearly, which would likely be part of the standard being addressed.

Time-Bound

Finally, objectives should be time-bound. It should be clear to students not only what is expected of them, but the time frame by which the expectation is to be fulfilled. This will not only help students manage their time more effectively, but it will also help the teacher to estimate the overall expenditure required by the unit. Often times, the "time boundary" for an objective is listed in the beginning of the actual phrasing of the objective. Examples of time-bound phrases include:

- By the end of this lesson
- By 10:30
- By the end of this class period
- By the end of the week

Once again, the time frames indicated are not prescriptive. In fact, we have found in our own teaching that the initial time frame listed for each objective is simply an informed estimate. There will certainly be instances in which a particular objective takes more time for students to explore. However, once a teacher has identified that the initial time frame is not accurate, it is important to set new parameters so that students are cognizant of the shift. We want to stress here that it is not imperative that SMART objectives be developed for the entire unit before teaching the unit. Based on the unit plan, teachers may decide that it is easier to develop SMART objectives for one lesson at a time. Remember, the overall unit is likely going to be comprised of several lessons and formative assessments that lead up to the summative assessment.

Selecting and Designing Appropriate Instructional Activities

As we stated previously, instruction must be purposeful and intentional. After the development of formative assessments and SMART objectives, it is now time to identify or design instructional strategies that will engage students in the learning process and enable them to be successful on the formative assessment. The key to effective instruction is choosing the right strategy, for the right purpose, at the right time. In order to ensure that the instructional strategies do indeed engage students in the acquisition of knowledge, we have developed three guiding questions to consider as one examines appropriate instructional strategies for an effective fit. It is our belief that an effective instructional strategy will allow you to answer "yes" to all three questions. If the strategy you are considering does not meet the criteria implied in any one of the questions, that would be an indication for modifying the activity so it provides a more effective fit with the instructional aims, or finding a new activity.

1. Does the instructional strategy bring students to the same level of Bloom's required by the SMART objective and formative assessment? This question challenges the instructional designer to ensure that the strategy utilizes the same level of Bloom's taxonomy as the objective. As previously discussed, standards not only ask students to perform certain tasks and think about various ideas, but they require students to "perform" and "think" at very specific levels of cognition. In order to align to standards, classroom instructional activities should reflect a similar level of cognition as that required by the standard. Bloom's taxonomy was introduced as a tool for determining the level of thinking required by a standard. Once a teacher has determined the level of cognition required by the standard, he or she can revisit Bloom's in order to determine whether the chosen instructional activity will require the corresponding level of rigor.

For example, one cannot expect students to master an objective that is at the analysis level in Bloom's (Level IV) if the classroom instruction merely provides students with foundational knowledge (Level I). The instructional strategies should provide opportunities for students to understand the content as well as challenge them at the exact cognitive level that they need to apply the content. Our goal with this question is to challenge teachers to think about the efficacy of their instructional strategies in terms of the standards and assessments in play. If we are not cognizant of the level of thinking required by the standards, then we cannot ensure that our classroom instruction is indeed preparing students to be successful. With the level of thinking in mind, we can then select or modify an instructional strategy as necessary to engage students at the appropriate level of thinking required by the standard.

Consider the following 7th-grade social studies standard that Mr. Flores is planning for: "Describe the importance of written and oral traditions in the transmission of African history and culture." After prioritizing this standard, Mr. Flores determined that it was a Level II (comprehension) skill and was also prioritized as P2. The formative assessment was a constructed response assessment in which students would write an essay explaining three reasons why the written and oral traditions were important. The SMART objective for this standard was, "By the end of the week, students will write a five-paragraph essay detailing three reasons why written and oral traditions were important in the transmission of African history and culture."

When delivering his instruction, Mr. Flores lectured on several written and oral traditions of African cultures. Additionally, he provided students with articles about various traditions applicable to the topic. In small groups, students read each article and summarized the traditions. Each group then presented their findings to the class. Using a graphic organizer, students took notes and by the end of the week had a comprehensive list of various written and oral traditions within African cultures.

When asking the guiding question, it should become clear that despite the level of thinking implied by the standard, the classroom instruction only required students to operate at Level I of Bloom's (knowledge). Students were never questioned as to why the traditions were important. Rather, Mr. Flores focused on the identification of specific traditions. A more effective instructional strategy would have asked the students not only to identify the different traditions but also examine and explain their importance within the context of African culture.

The strategies Mr. Flores used were not "bad" strategies—they were just inappropriate and inadequate to the instructional goals in this case. By utilizing the guiding question, Mr. Flores could have readily modified his instructional strategies to ensure that students moved beyond Level I and into Level II.

The point of this entire process, particularly at this stage, is to enable teachers to think critically about their instructional strategies and to determine how or why they should modify a strategy, if the guiding question reveals the need to do so. Again, we know that there are countless strategies that can be used to teach a single topic. However, in order for the strategy to be effective, teachers must first understand what the standard requires of students and then select a strategy that will enable students to meet or exceed the stated standards.

2. Does the strategy facilitate the acquisition of knowledge/skills in a way that can be applied to accomplish the standard? So often in our classrooms, we expect that students will fully understand a topic once it has been explained by the teacher. What this approach fails to take into account is that students need an opportunity to actually engage in a meaningful exploration of the content. The premise of this question is once again that teachers should be aware that they must be facilitators of knowledge and skills, rather than mere deliverers of "the truth" to students. Once teachers think about their instructional role as that of a facilitator, the shift in thinking greatly impacts which instructional strategies are chosen and the way they are utilized.

Let us examine a 3rd-grade math standard that states: "Determine the unit cost when given the total cost and number of units." After walking this standard through the prioritization process, the teacher determined that this was a Level III (application) and a P2. As her formative assessment required, the teacher had created a classroom supply order form that listed the item, the number of units ordered, and the total cost. The SMART objective she created was, "By the end of the math period, students will be able to find the unit price of three items from the classroom supply order form." From this, she would ask students to determine the cost for a single pencil, a math book, and a desk.

Now let us examine her instructional strategies in relation to the task on the assessment. It would be very easy for the teacher to give a lesson, ask the students to work some practice division problems, and then hand them the formative assessment. After all, students need to know how to divide in order to determine the unit cost when given the total cost and number of units. However, a lesson on division only requires students to know and comprehend the concept of division. In order to accomplish the objective, students must also be able to apply this knowledge in another context, in this case, the classroom supply order form. A more appropriate instructional strategy would be an exercise in which the teacher provided practice in the skill of determining unit costs using a similar process, such as determining how much an orange costs if a woman bought five oranges for $1.20. The teacher might have used centers with different activities, had students work in small groups to accomplish the task, or even had students create their own order forms. The bottom line is that any of these strategies is a better match to the objective than an activity that merely engages students in the practice of division of numbers without the application of the skill to another context.

For example, if we expect students to write a hypothesis, we cannot assume that they will be able to do this by merely hearing the teacher tell the class what a hypothesis is. Effective instructional strategies will engage students in the process of fully understanding what a hypothesis is in order to be able to generate one of their own. Students must know what the parts of a viable hypothesis are, why one generates a hypothesis, and how it relates to the query at hand. In this instance, classroom instruction should engage students in tasks that allow them to explore the parts of a hypothesis, break apart good and bad examples of hypotheses, and practice writing hypotheses with constructive feedback from peers or the teacher. In short, classroom instruction must involve more than merely giving students the content. The instruction must engage students in a manner that provides them with an opportunity to practice the intended task, based on instruction and modeling by the teacher. With this question, we want teachers to think about process in the classroom. How will students be required to process the content within the objective, and what processes are most efficacious for the objective?

3. Do the instructional strategies account for a diversity of ability levels and learning styles? When sorting through the many available activities and instructional resources, teachers should consider whether the activity can be adapted to meet the needs of diverse learners. When examining an instructional activity, teachers may want to ask themselves questions such as these:

- Can less skilled readers get the information they need in some nonwritten way?
- Does the activity address the needs of auditory, visual, and kinesthetic learners?
- Will English language learners be able to access the content?
- Are there opportunities for students to work independently and in groups on this activity?
- Can this activity be extended to challenge advanced learners?

These are just a few of the many issues teachers must consider with any instructional activity. Carol Ann Tomlinson (2001), a leader in the field

of differentiated instruction, succinctly summarizes some the key understandings in the field about effective instruction. Essentially, she articulates
a need for teachers to understand that learning takes place in classrooms
where knowledge is clearly and powerfully organized, when the learning
experience pushes the learner a bit beyond his or her independence level,
and when students feel a kinship with, interest in, or passion for what
they are attempting to learn.

In order for the conditions that Tomlinson describes to exist, teachers
cannot operate in a one-size-fits-all mode of instruction. Rather, as described by Tomlinson, "Teachers need to constantly seek ways to create a
variety of ways students can gather information and ideas, develop varied
ways students can explore their own ideas, and present varied channels
through which students can express and expand understandings" (p. 16).

Our purpose here is not to reinvent the wheel of differentiated instruction, which has been so eloquently defined and actualized by Tomlinson
and other scholars. Rather, we seek to remind teachers to privilege student
needs as a driving force in instructional design.

MS. KWON REVISITED

Now that we have presented the entire Strategic Design model, let us revisit Ms. Kwon, from Chapter 1, as she begins planning her unit on the
digestive system 1 year later. Remember our initial inquiry: *How can teachers like Ms. Kwon retain creative control over their instructional design while
ensuring that students attain mastery of content standards?* As Ms. Kwon attempted to resolve this dilemma, her realizations concerning the reasons
why her students had failed to achieve on the district benchmark exams
have challenged her to consider how she might address digestion differently—without losing the student engagement that is the hallmark of her
classroom.

Guided by the Strategic Design process, Ms. Kwon considered the following questions as she planned her new unit on the digestive system:

- What are the standards asking of my students?
- How might I examine the standards to determine what is expected
  of the students?
- Does the assessment specific to the classroom lesson, in this case
  the dissection, actually assess student knowledge of the digestive
  system that is required by the relevant standards?
- How might I redesign my assessment to enable students to
  demonstrate mastery of the related standards?

- What type of classroom instruction will prepare students for the summative assessment?

Ms. Kwon's new strategically designed unit on the digestive system was remarkably successful in addressing these critical issues. During her reexamination of the content standards, she realized that the standards required students to know about each of the elements of the digestive system as well as their role in the overall digestion process—a much deeper understanding of the digestive system than she had originally demanded from her students.

Thus, before engaging in instructional strategies she would use to teach the digestive system, Ms. Kwon first thought about the ways in which she could effectively assess student mastery of the standards, as well as communicate to the students the level of understanding of the digestive system that was expected of them. She was aware of student enthusiasm for the dissection project, and decided to retain it while modifying it to make it even more effective. In addition to dissecting the frog and labeling the parts of the digestive system, now the students would also be required to complete a constructed response assessment that accompanied the project. In sum, the test questions asked the students to list the parts of the digestive system and then describe the role of each. Ms. Kwon created a thorough rubric as well as an example of what a high-quality project would look like. (In order to avoid feeling like she was giving the students the answers, her exemplar was developed around the respiratory system.) Again, by providing the unit objectives and assessment exemplar prior to beginning instruction, she made her students aware of the expectations up front. They knew that in addition to knowing the parts of the digestive system, they would also be required to write about the specific role of each part in relation to the system as a whole.

Finally, her classroom instruction engaged students in the work of truly learning about the digestive system. Ms. Kwon utilized direct instruction, cooperative learning, and independent practice to teach the concepts embedded in the standards. Throughout the 3-week unit, students had continuous opportunities to demonstrate their knowledge of the standards. For example, students kept journals in which they wrote definitions of the parts of the digestive system, took notes from class discussions, and wrote down their thoughts about new discoveries about the digestive system. Both as a class and individually, they practiced writing about how specific parts of the digestive system functioned. They played "Digestive System Jeopardy," created models of the digestive system, and wrote a letter to a friend from the perspective of one part of the digestive system about what they do all day. Needless to say, at the end of the 3 weeks, students were deeply engaged in their learning and Ms. Kwon was much more confident that her students were actually meeting the standards.

At the end of the unit, Ms. Kwon invited the principal to view her students' completed dissection projects. The projects themselves, along with the constructed response assessment, provided explicit evidence that students had indeed mastered the standards. We utilize the example of Ms. Kwon to illustrate that the Strategic Design process provides a method and a guiding framework for a teacher's instructional practices, without forcing teachers to surrender their classrooms and their professional and pedagogical independence to prepackaged programs. Ms. Kwon's example demonstrates that teachers can maintain professional integrity while ensuring that students can master standards in an era of accountability.

CHAPTER 5

Lessons Learned

THE IMPORTANCE OF REFLECTION

As we were working on this book, we had several discussions about how best to engage the concept of reflection within it. Initially, we had thought to include it as a part of our instruction chapter, but what we struggled with the most was the fact that reflection plays a part in every aspect of the Strategic Design process, and not with regard to instruction alone. Consequently, we thought of discussing reflection throughout the text, but we did not want to distract the reader from the task at hand, which was a clear and concise understanding of the various stages of the Strategic Design process.

Thus, given the evolution of the book, we thought this chapter, aptly titled "Lessons Learned," was an appropriate place to discuss our concept of reflection, with the hope that you will be left with the salient arguments about the importance of being a reflective learner as well as a reflective teacher. Reflection is an essential component of the Strategic Design process, and in order to become a reflective teacher, one must first learn to function as a reflective learner. In relating some of our ideas on reflection, we refer to the work of Jack Mezirow (1991), a consequential thinker and theoretician in the field of adult learning. In considering the process of adult learning, Mezirow places a critical emphasis on attempting to understand *how* adults make meaning and sense from their contextualized experiences. He surmises that adults must be able to engage in critical reflection of their assumptions, and gain validity of what is meaningful to them by understanding the reasoning behind their meaning-making processes. Similarly, we feel that the Strategic Design process, as it has been envisioned and presented here, continually asks us to reflect on the "why" of our actions as opposed to just the "how."

It is no secret that designing effective classroom instruction and then executing it successfully is a process that is in a constant state of flux. Because there are no surefire lesson plans, even the best instructional strategies can turn out to be ineffective when materially deployed in the classroom. Within the dynamics and premise of Strategic Design, such occasional failures should not be cause for worry or distress. Rather, we take them as signs of a vigorous and active classroom that is constantly evolving. It is our belief that such moments of "failure" should be utilized to examine our pedagogical processes with a critical eye—perhaps this best describes and inscribes what we mean by reflection.

We have consistently insisted on the concept of the "reflective practitioner" as a necessary part of thoughtful instructional design. Reflection enables us to identify what is productive and enabling for our students. While there are stages in the Strategic Design process that are particularly conducive to reflection, especially as we invoke the term and the concept, reflection within Strategic Design is really an ongoing evaluation and dialogue (both with colleagues and oneself) that the teacher/learner is engaged in to promote the intellectual growth of all stakeholders.

During the process of instructional design and delivery, it is important that one reflect upon the lesson—its structure, content, and delivery—in order to evaluate its effectiveness and make changes for the future. Being a reflective practitioner is not just about determining what "worked" and what didn't, or even striving to understand *why* a lesson was successful or ineffective. The reflective practitioner is one who constantly attempts to understand and be open to learning yet again the dynamics of the classroom and the pedagogical processes that define that classroom. It is only when we examine our practice with this level of depth that we can have the type of instruction our students deserve.

This request on our part to engage in reflection may, at first glance, appear to be yet another step in an already complex and seemingly overburdened process. We fully understand that designing instruction is already extremely time-consuming, and often frustrating. And as always, we are cognizant that the one thing teachers have very little of is time. We are confident, however, that productively engaging in reflection assists a teacher in internalizing the process of designing and implementing instructional strategies. We also want to point out that our repeated insistence on internalizing what we do in the classroom has not been suggested lightly, but rather as something that we take very seriously because of the depth it adds to the complex and continuous negotiation that is effective instruction.

The Reflective Learner

We must consider reflection in terms of how it impacts one's ability to accept and internalize the process of instructional design, and also in terms of how reflecting on the design impacts future instruction. As individuals, we must first learn to reflect in terms of our own learning before we can become adept at reflecting as a professional. In this context, we are specifically referring to one's ability to reflect upon the content presented in this book, and the material presented interacts with one's existing frame(s) of reference.

Contemporary theories on adult learning, premised on the concept of *transformative learning*, place a critical importance on individuals' critical assessment and reassessment of the values, thoughts, experiences, knowledge, and skills that construct their current perspectives and serve as both the foundation and catalyst for their actions. Jack Mezirow, who is a consequential thinker on the dynamics of adult learning, shares a fundamental philosophy and belief with other theoreticians in the field that our emerging understanding of learning needs to encompass an element of critical reflection to enable an increased awareness of one's thoughts, feelings, values, and actions. Endemic to this concept is the notion that to create meaningful and *enduring* change, it is necessary for individuals and groups to discard those accepted "realities" that undermine growth and strive to make meaning and sense of new perceptions.

Similarly, we feel that in order to be fully open to the possibilities enabled by Strategic Design, teachers must transform their own thinking about the process of instructional design. Throughout this book, we have repeatedly asserted that each and every individual brings expertise and experience to the process of instructional planning, and we hope that this assertion confirms our foundational premise that instruction is dynamic, evolving, and not conducive to magic formulas and prescribed scripts. Consequently, it is important to point out that we are not advocating for a complete abandonment of one's current beliefs in favor of ours, for such a desire would be counter to our valuing individual teachers and the experiences they bring to the classroom. However, we do believe that reflection on one's pedagogical practices, while engaging in the process of understanding and utilizing Strategic Design, will empower teachers to transform their approach to planning classroom instruction in an ideal way.

Another central practice, in our opinion, is to engage in reflection via collegial dialogue. This is the reason we have engaged in the quest to design a truly collaborative and exploratory professional development model. We have learned so much from talking to each other, our colleagues, and the teachers we work with. We deliberately design our trainings to allow time for focused dialogue. We understand the value of dialogue with colleagues—and we love to see discussion and debate that are informed by experience and challenged by new learning and other people. Given our extensive fieldwork experience, we can say without hesitation that reflection, in our opinion, is a personal and professional necessity. Sometimes our own reflection is provoked by questions, and there have even been times when the questions we have been asked have had an element of confrontation in them. However, we embrace this dialogic process as a means for our own reflection and growth, as well as an opportunity for individuals to explore their own beliefs in relation to what they have learned. Just as students benefit from engaging in collaborative learning experiences with their classmates, so, too, do teachers benefit from dialogue as reflection. Mezirow refers to this process as communicative learning. In addition to understanding the content of new knowledge, communicative learning requires an interpretation of another's assumptions, objectives, meanings, values, and unarticulated innuendo of dialogue. A combination of both types of learning is necessary if transformation is to occur. One must not only understand and become competent in the "mechanics" of a particular entity, but must also be able to critically analyze, interpret, and validate the authenticity of the assumptions, thus prompting the individual to become critically reflective.

The Reflective Teacher

It is only after an individual is able to engage in reflection as a learner that he or she can engage in the process of being a reflective teacher. Reflective teaching is the examination of teaching practices both before and after the teaching of lessons in an effort to continually evolve as a professional and become a more effective teacher. Although some might rightfully argue that the idea of continuous improvement has been overused and oversimplified in the context of education, it is nevertheless a powerful concept, and by no means do we feel that the ideal of the premise should be dismissed. Both as advisors and teachers ourselves, being open to the process of evolving to improve, in our experience, enables the best and most effective teaching. In an era of changing expectations and increased challenges, it is imperative that we begin to develop communities of reflective teachers. Our students deserve it.

Reflective teachers examine their effectiveness when prioritizing standards, designing assessments, and planning instructional activities. Throughout the process that we have attempted to bring to life through this book, the most effective teachers engage in the application of the content to their own practice through constant reflection. Because of the habits we form, we must make a concerted effort to move away from the pattern of teaching, testing, and moving on. In his writings, Mezirow asserts that our frames of reference are integrally aligned with a "self"—what one believes they are. Against this assumption of a self that we believe to be valid and unchanging, Mezirow suggests that "we may transform our habit of the mind by becoming critically reflective of our premises in defining the problem, such as by questioning the validity of our assumptions" (1991, p. 20). Therefore, individuals and groups must be willing to reform the vision, mission, systems, and practices that they have become accustomed to, in order to enhance performance. As with all theories that project an evolution in stages, Mezirow admits that the exacting moments that might illustrate the progress of an individual's journey toward transformation will be illusive, fluid, and difficult to capture, but that does not mean that the journey is not worth our efforts.

Thus we must continuously reflect upon our lessons and the myriad and interacting processes of our pedagogy—look at student engagement and assessment results—and through this thorough (self) examination, gain the knowledge that allows us to productively engage in re-vision as necessary. In short, we must be willing to admit that perhaps we might have done something better—and then be willing to do what we need to do to make the improvements necessary to give our students what they really deserve.

LESSONS LEARNED FROM AN AMAZING SCHOOL

Over the years, we have also spent a great deal of time reflecting upon how the schools we have worked with have stepped up to the challenge of creating high-quality learning environments for the students they serve. Some schools will always be more poised to adopt our approach, or have a more genuine enthusiasm for the approach we take to instructional design, and consequently the work we do. Some schools we have worked with have taken our model and made it their own, using it as a tool to guide the development of curriculum and improve student achievement. The culture of the school and the groundwork of school leadership require that this model be flexible enough to accommodate very different school communities. In the ideal situation, Strategic Design is only one part of a larger program for school success. We suppose the happiest lesson learned is that our concept of how Strategic Design can indeed create a new kind of school has been materially realized. We are speaking of the work we have done at Livermore.

Livermore Valley Charter School (LVCS) in Livermore, California, is a K–8 school of 700 students. With effective leadership, dedicated teachers, and a clear commitment to the development of teachers as professionals, this school has implemented Strategic Design more effectively than one could have imagined. After only 1 year of implementation, the staff at the school had worked to develop high-quality units that were relevant and aligned to standards. However, and perhaps more importantly, they learned what questions to ask and how to work collaboratively to develop a curriculum program that is intentional and intelligent.

Our process began with a 5-day professional development session called the Instructional Design Academy. During those 5 days, grade-level teams were trained in the Strategic Design process. By the end of the week, each grade level had prioritized their content standards and clustered them. The process, although intended to train a group of teachers on the process, was also deliberately designed to allow teachers time to build collaborative teams that would work together for the entire year.

As the school year opened, teachers were committed to implementing their new units and to showing their students their new approach to classroom instruction. It did not take long for many to realize, however, that they had only taken the first step in a long and intensive learning journey. Each grade level learned that implementing such units, and acclimating their students to this new curricular approach, would take some time. After all, many of these teachers had been effectively teaching for a number of years. And although they had theoretically bought in to the approach, old habits die hard.

We spent between 2 and 4 days each month working with the principal, grade-level teams, and individual teachers to refine their teaching practices. During these days of coaching, grade-level leads would let us know what each team was working on. Most often we would meet with each grade-level team and facilitate the development of a unit or the analysis of an assessment, or help them identify instructional strategies aligned to their assessments. At the end of each visit, we would frequently set a goal for the team or individual to accomplish before our next visit.

In addition to coaching, we had the opportunity to work with the staff to adopt math textbooks, create standards-based report cards, work to implement Individual Learning Plans that were aligned to the standards, and learn from some of the best teachers in the country. Each month we would enjoy seeing the significant growth of the curricular culture of the school. In the lunchroom teachers frequently talked about their instruction, supporting individual students, or trying to figure out which curricular resources would support their units.

Although this passage may make LVCS look like a dream school, we want to be very clear that what was most impressive was that teachers were consistently engaged in high-level thinking and hard work. They were stressed, frustrated, and annoyed at times. They became tired, skeptical, and tempted to give up. However, the school principal and grade-level teams had developed a culture in which they could motivate one another to continue on the journey of continuous improvement. And the engagement of their students continued to remind them of why they were working so hard.

Many have asked us how we made it work. And as much as we would love to take credit for their success, it is quite clear that it is a combination of effective leadership, committed teachers, and a very well-thought out plan for training and support that elicited the results we are all so proud of.

Most impressive is the fact that if you step on this campus today and ask teachers about the process, they will immediately begin to list all the work that still needs to be done. They will impress upon you the fact that as soon as they think they are perfect teachers, they will be failing to serve their students and grow as professionals. And their principal brilliantly learned along with her teachers and allocated appropriate resources to ensure that her teachers were supported in order to continue their growth. An effective team with a focused plan and a commitment to succeed will accomplish great things.

We have always known that a successful program aimed at increasing student achievement is a significant undertaking that requires a substantial investment of time and energy. Without ongoing support and collaboration, and the acceptance that any substantial transformation needs time (sometimes 3 to 5 years) to achieve full implementation, any program will fall flat. We have learned that we must be extremely thoughtful in how we initiate school reform. It must involve teachers from its very inception and throughout the entire process. And most importantly, the conversation must always revolve around what is best for kids.

We have not developed Strategic Design to tell you how to be a teacher, or what kind of a teacher to be. Our goal and purpose is to support teachers in their quest to accommodate the need for standards-based instruction without sacrificing the feelings of why we became teachers in the first place—a love for children, a desire to be creative with classroom instruction, and a need for some independence within the context of a larger school community.

CHAPTER 6

Conclusion

Strategic Design for Student Achievement is about creating great classrooms for our students. And although we have stated this before, we feel it is worth repeating: Put simply, Strategic Design is a way of thinking. The process combines all the critical aspects of teaching into a workable praxis that teachers can make their own by calling upon their own experiences and needs. No doubt, as the previous pages demonstrate, the implementation of Strategic Design as a process is not easy—hard work and extensive thinking are required. Teachers need to engage in thoroughly and systematically analyzing standards, and aligning classroom assessments and instruction to those standards. We feel that the special value of the Strategic Design process lies in the fact that the process treats teachers as professionals, and is indeed reliant upon teachers utilizing their own experiences and creativity to think about instructional design in a different way.

Of course, with such creative control comes added responsibility. Teachers must embrace the process and dedicate the time and energy to design curriculum or analyze existing resources, utilizing a field-tested design process. This provides us with the opportunity to improve our teaching skills, and ultimately provide learning environments in which students consistently meet grade-level expectations and find success.

We have often been asked how Strategic Design is different or what makes this approach worthy of attention. And although we readily acknowledge that there are many published works in the field full of great ideas and effective approaches to instruction, this work has been informed by the users of the model. The lengthy development process of this book has enabled us to make revisions prior to this publication, bringing about a stronger final product informed by the teachers who have used the process. Perhaps more importantly, we are able to present the reader with a book that was essentially "co-written" by hundreds of current classroom teachers doing amazing things with kids.

Today, standards-based reform efforts expect teachers to utilize assessment methods to assess student mastery of content knowledge specific to content standards. Consequently, Strategic Design is a standards-based instructional planning model. That is, it is completely reliant upon the use of standards. Strategic Design, as you have learned through reading this book, is really a way to authentically embed standards into the planning process, and the process itself would not exist without standards. We have worked to provide a way for teachers to interact with the standards in a way that feels not only productive, but leads to an instructional program that moves students toward content mastery.

In today's climate, many teachers do not consider themselves to be curriculum designers. Rather, they view themselves as deliverers of an already established curriculum. This is a function of the expectations that have been set forth for teachers. In light of the overwhelming research that identifies the teacher as the single biggest factor in affecting student achievement, we feel it is time for these long-existing expectations to change. Effective teachers are much more than just deliverers of instruction. Effective teachers do not simply pick up a textbook, start from page one, and move through the entire book without constantly checking to see if the students understand the concepts being presented, while adjusting the way in which the concepts are presented based on student learning styles. Effective teachers do not simply obtain instructional strategies from the Internet or strategy manuals and use them in their classrooms without first thinking about how that strategy aligns to the intended learning priority and how it will be assessed. Nor do good teachers simply accept the instructional strategies presented in a textbook. Effective teachers scrutinize these strategies to determine how well they will work within the given context of their classroom. Such context takes into account student readiness, learning styles, and interests as well as the value of the strategy in leading students toward the intended outcome.

Achieving effective instruction is difficult, complex, and time-consuming work. However, it is work that we believe must be done in order to raise the level of the teaching profession and to close the achievement gap. Trying to actualize the concept of "backward design" (Wiggins & McTighe, 2005) that seems so right to us is what motivated us to develop the Strategic Design process.

What we have learned as teachers and now as professionals in the field working with teachers is the acknowledgment that there is no single formula for creating standards-based, differentiated classrooms. All teaching must be guided by the needs of the learners. Essentially, what we discovered is that when the first two stages of Strategic Design are done effectively, aligning instructional strategies according to the specifics of a classroom can be quite easy.

As you have witnessed in the previous pages, Strategic Design utilizes three stages that are involved in planning backward. The three stages are labeled as follows: (1) identify learning priorities, (2) align assessments, and (3) design instruction.

THE THREE STAGES OF STRATEGIC DESIGN

Stage One

The intended outcome for stage one of Strategic Design is the identification of learning priorities. First, Strategic Design asks teachers to derive learning priorities solely from the content standards.

Second, Strategic Design utilizes a multistep process to help teachers analyze content standards and derive learning priorities. We found that when we asked teachers to engage in a multistep analysis process to identify learning priorities within content standards, it was important to represent that process in a concrete, linear manner for ease of use and reference. Thus we invented the flow chart that represents the analysis and prioritization process in a step-by-step, easy-to-follow graphic. In our initial work with teachers we provided several graphic organizers compiled in a workbook to help teachers engage in the analysis process. Even with these graphic organizers, we found that teachers would often not work through the process in a systematic fashion, but rather would rely on their own initial judgment or intuition about standards to identify learning priorities, even after modeling and discussing each step of the process. In an effort not to keep the analysis process from being circumvented, we needed to find a way to direct teachers back to the specific steps of the process. The flow chart provided the redirection we were looking for and has become the hallmark of Stage One of the Strategic Design process.

We also found that teachers needed a concrete starting point to engage in their analysis of standards. In the Strategic Design process, that starting point is Bloom's taxonomy. Bloom's taxonomy provides a very concrete schema that teachers use to begin to analyze learning priorities (standards).

In addition, Bloom's taxonomy plays a critical role in the remaining two stages of the Strategic Design process. It is the common denominator between all three stages of the process. For example, our goal in aligning assessments to standards is for teachers to think about what concrete, visible evidence students will produce to demonstrate mastery of the standard. The most direct link to find that appropriate evidence, in our opinion, is through Bloom's taxonomy. Additionally, since we spend so much time using Bloom's in the examination of content standards, it only makes sense that we continue using this tool to ensure the entire instructional design program is aligned. The foundation of our model is the examination of the levels of thinking required by the standards in order to ensure student success. By also aligning assessments to the standards using Bloom's, we are able to ensure a tight alignment.

We felt it was important to provide some sort of schema that could help teachers explicitly link the three stages of the Strategic Design process together. This explicit link helps unify the stages of the process so that teachers can more concretely see the connections between standards, assessment, and instruction. This unifying link is unique to the Strategic Design process.

Stage Two

As we state above, Bloom's taxonomy serves as the common denominator that links all three stages of the Strategic Design process. The specific link between Stages One and Two is as follows: In Stage One of Strategic Design we ask teachers, as part of the analysis process, to label standards with the level(s) of thinking in Bloom's taxonomy required by the standard. During Stage Two, we revisit these labels and ask teachers to think about the assessment method that would serve as the most efficient and effective concrete measure of that type of thinking. It is often at this stage in the process that the proverbial lightbulbs begin to turn on in teachers' heads because they start to see the explicit connection between standards and the four assessment methods.

Stage Three

Stage Three of the backward design process deals with day-to-day classroom instruction. At this stage, teachers are deciding which instructional strategies would best be suited for the intended outcome(s) of a lesson or unit, and they use Bloom's taxonomy once again to identify an appropriate instructional strategy.

One of the primary considerations we ask teachers to think about is, what level of thinking (again in Bloom's taxonomy) does the chosen strategy require students to operate within? The key question at this stage is, "Does the instructional strategy provide students with an opportunity to practice the skills and acquire the knowledge that will enable them to be successful on the assessment?" With this question in mind, teachers once again make the explicit link between standards, assessment, and instruction via Bloom's taxonomy. While we encourage teachers to consider research-based instructional strategies, we also place a high premium on not simply accepting the strategy and using it for the sake of using a research-based strategy. It must align to the assessment and standard for the given lesson or unit.

THE RATIONALE FOR STRATEGIC DESIGN

As educators are well aware, in an era of standards and accountability, the field of education is not short on instructional strategies. One can find thousands of lesson plans on almost any topic. Our goal through the three stages summarized above and elaborated in the previous chapters of the book is to streamline the best of those resources in order to provide a vehicle for great teaching and learning. In fact, we would argue that one of the greatest downfalls of most reform movements lies in a school's attempts to implement several of the "best research-based programs" at once. Strategic Design is a direct response to this dilemma. Our quest over the past several years has been to build a model of instructional design that is *informed* by the best thinking in the field without taking away the craft of teaching by "overprescribing" or overwhelming classrooms and the teachers who facilitate the learning in these classrooms. As we were developing Strategic Design, we discovered that if we are clear about the level of cognition required by the standard, and we know how we will assess student mastery, identifying appropriate instructional strategies becomes a much easier task.

Of course, we acknowledge the power of some of the valuable scholarship that exists on instructional strategies—indeed, our work is indebted to such scholarship—and we encourage teachers to use and consider the work that has been done on instructional strategies. However, as we have stated throughout this book, Strategic Design places a premium on considering the context in which these strategies are used by teachers in the classroom. Strategic Design assumes that these strategies may be useful in facilitating student learning. However, if that student learning is not directed toward a specific outcome, then the time spent using these strategies in the classroom is wasted. The learning priority (standards) must be identified and clarified first, and an assessment mechanism must be articulated, before a strategy can be chosen that would best suit the purpose of teaching to that learning priority. Unless a teacher has fully analyzed the standards and identified the level of thinking (Bloom's taxonomy) a standard requires, it is quite possible that a teacher might use a teaching strategy to promote a level of thinking among students that is inconsistent with the level of thinking required by a standard. For example, unless a teacher identifies the purpose of homework assigned and identifies what type of skills are called into play by that homework, then such a teaching strategy could very well turn into nothing more than busywork for students. Anytime a teacher is directing a student, it should be clear to all (teacher, students, parents) how the specific task will allow the student an opportunity to gain facility in the types of skills or knowledge that will be needed to do well on the assessment and demonstrate mastery of the learning priority (standards). The Strategic Design process helps teachers analyze teaching strategies in relation to the context within which they are to be used (particularly in the third stage of the process) in order to help teachers make good decisions about how to use instructional strategies effectively.

TEACHER RESPONSES TO STRATEGIC DESIGN

We have been in the field for quite some time now presenting Strategic Design to teachers, and have a clear sense from the teacher responses as to what aspects of the program have been most beneficial in the classroom. When asked what they felt were the most important things to include in the book, teachers consistently shared a few key takeaways.

First, many feel as if Strategic Design finally helped them grasp the salient aspects of much of the field theory through a practical application of it. Comments like this tell us that we have achieved the correct balance. The concept of backward planning is by no means new to the field. In fact, many of the teachers we work with have commented that they learned about the concept of backward design in their credentialing programs or in professional development, and thus they had initially thought that Strategic Design might be repetitious and a waste of their time. However, after experiencing the Strategic Design process firsthand, these same teachers would invariably comment that while they had learned about the concept of backward design on a theoretical level, they had never learned how to actually apply the concept in their classrooms, given the unique context each classroom presents. Once they have been exposed to Strategic Design, new and veteran teachers alike always say that they now feel empowered to actually develop lessons in a backward fashion. The goal of Strategic Design is, and always has been, to empower teachers to take back control of instructional design with the intent of providing high-quality instruction for all students.

Another comment that closely relates to the one above is that teachers feel that the Strategic Design process, once executed in the classrooms, allows "students to understand the 'why' of what they are learning." One of the most significant outcomes of the Strategic Design process is that teachers design and deliver lessons that facilitate student understanding regarding why a particular subject, content, or skill is being taught in the classroom. If a teacher keeps this concept at the forefront of everything he or she does, then we truly believe that the attitudes and conversations that fill classrooms will be much richer and deeper than those that result from the "I have to" or "because I said so" mentality.

After learning about Strategic Design, many teachers have commented that they finally feel they have a concrete sense of direction on how to use the standards, and they no longer feel constrained by them. In our fieldwork it is not surprising to find that teachers often harbor an initial resentment toward standards because they approach standards not as something that can guide their instruction, but rather as a top-down mandate they have been asked to teach to. This top-down directive often alienates teachers because their first reaction is that they are losing control of their ability to make professional decisions in the classroom. Obviously, when standards are viewed almost as a punitive measure, teachers quickly lose interest in working with them. Much of our time has been spent having professional conversations about standards, their intent, the hurdles in implementing them, and how to overcome these hurdles while maintaining creative control in the classroom. We do not advocate that standards can or should be taught in the same way in every classroom. The teacher plays a huge role in determining how to deliver the standards to students in order to appeal to different interests, learning modalities, and readiness levels. The Strategic Design process becomes a vehicle for having conversations about these kinds of things, and teachers respect and appreciate the fact that we treat them like professionals and honor their training, experience, and knowledge of their students' needs.

Believe it or not, improving teaching practice is possible—we have witnessed it. When we acknowledge the brilliance of teachers and actually provide the necessary supports for improvement, teachers are very willing to work hard on behalf of their students. Current approaches to accountability, while acknowledging the need for smarter children, have failed to provide the structures necessary for the ongoing and comprehensive professional development of teachers. Current accountability systems have simply said "it needs to happen"—without truly understanding or articulating what "it" really is.

Insightful district officials and school principals have leveraged their resources and developed professional learning communities in which professional development and support is instrumental in shaping classroom practice. Teachers are receiving several days of training in the summer and ongoing support throughout the school year. They work to dissect standards, align classroom assessments, and identify the most effective instructional strategies to ensure student mastery of the learning objectives found within content standards. Importantly, accountability is implemented in relation to benchmarks of teacher learning. Teachers are held accountable for mastering their own learning and meeting mutually developed expectations of curriculum development and implementation. School administrators use accountability tools to identify what elements of a teacher's practice do not meet expectations, and then *design supports for assisting the teacher in attaining mastery.* Good accountability for teachers should look like good classroom instruction. Teacher learning should be as critical to administrators as student learning. When appropriate attention, time, and money are devoted to enhancing the knowledge of our teachers, increased student achievement follows quite naturally.

As we have been discussing, Strategic Design is first and foremost a tool to address and navigate the complex arena of standards in a way that yields productive and results-oriented classrooms. Consequently, teachers who work with Strategic Design feel most positive about the opportunity to interact with standards on a practical level. Many teachers have also remarked that through the Strategic Design process, they get to understand standards in a practical way, with time built in for exploration, and that the process takes away the sense of threat that standards can sometimes represent. The level of comprehension about standards that can be achieved through Strategic Design is possible because we do not mire the standards in notions of accountability alone, but primarily as an opportunity to get to know what the standards are really asking of students, and how teachers as professionals can deliver the instruction that reflects that.

POSITIONING OURSELVES TODAY AND IN THE FUTURE

We want to continue to build learning environments that value the skills and experiences that teachers bring to the table—and even more importantly, provide opportunities for teachers to learn from one another. We are determined to provide a high-quality model of instructional design that really works—for everyone involved. And while we would never assert that Strategic Design is the be-all and end-all of classroom instruction, we do think that it is a well-thought-out and highly effective way to think about designing instruction.

We sincerely hope that our work provides a platform upon which schools can redefine the instructional culture of the school. The process can provide the overarching structure for other reforms at all levels of stakeholders to engage in. Strategic Design functions best when it is contextualized within a school culture committed to improving instructional quality. What we do necessarily deals with several different levels of the school, even if we do not have the ability to materially impact those levels through the workshops alone. We hope to have the opportunity to explore how Strategic Design, as a model of thinking, might transform principal effectiveness, teacher credentialing programs, and schoolwide decisionmaking. We think there is the potential to explore how we think about whole-school reform without losing the fact that instructional design must sit at the center of this discussion. One cannot improve classroom practice unless school structures are there to support that, so we have to work on many levels.

As our own next level of growth comes upon us, we envision implementing school structures that are inherently created to accommodate work like the Strategic Design process. We have been doing a lot of thinking recently on creating systemic models for school reform: How do you take existing schools and redesign them, or create new schools that are prepared to do something meaningful with a process like Strategic Design, so it can impact the whole school? We hope that we can continue to learn from our current experiences and have a significant impact on how schools provide opportunities for students to be successful, in school and beyond.

As we reflect upon our work in the field, we remember the amazing teachers who so effectively enlighten their students. We have said repeatedly that teachers have the greatest impact on student achievement, and it is time for us, as educators, to do all we can to ensure that students are getting everything they need to be successful, in school and in life. The field must continue to engage in a reflective process in which we do more than identify what is not working and point fingers or place blame. It is time for us to celebrate those teachers who engage in the challenging work of ensuring that their students are learning. It is time for us to celebrate those teachers and schools who engage in reflection and instructional design with the goal of increasing student achievement.

We look forward to being part of a field of professionals who, on a very real level, work to shape the future of our country. As quotidian as this may sound, it is very real. And until we as a profession understand that this is true, we will never have the impact that is needed. We hope, as teachers and now authors, that we have contributed to the field in a substantial way. Strategic Design was born out of a desire to become better teachers and provide an accessible instructional design model for other teachers to engage in. We hope this book has done just that.

References and Relevant Literature

American Federation of Teachers. (2001). *Making standards matter 2001* [Electronic Version]. Retrieved July 3, 2004, from http://65.110.81.56/pubs-reports/downloads/teachers/msm2001.pdf

Anderson, S. E. (2003). *The school district role in educational change: A review of the literature* [Working Paper #2, International Centre for Educational Change]. Ontario: Ontario Institute for Studies in Education.

Arter, J. A., & Busick, K. U. (2001). *Practice with student-involved classroom assessment.* Portland, OR: Assessment Training Institute.

Berliner, D. C. (1993, April). Mythology and the American system of education. *Phi Delta Kappan, 74*(8), 632–640.

Betts, J. R., Zau, A. C., & Rice, L. A. (2003). *Determinants of student achievement: New evidence from San Diego.* San Francisco: Public Policy Institute of California. Retrieved September 30, 2003, from http://ppic.org/content/pubs/r803JBR.pdf

Black, P., & William, D. (1998). Inside the black box: Raising standards through classroom assessment. *Phi Delta Kappan, 80*(2), 139–148.

Bloom, B. S. (1956). *Taxonomy of educational objectives, Handbook I: The cognitive domain.* New York: David McKay.

Bolman, L., & Deal, T. (1997). *Reframing organizations: Artistry, choice, and leadership.* San Francisco: Jossey-Bass.

Brennan, A. (2001). A comprehensive paper on staff development. *Articles & Resources on Educational Administration & Supervision.* Retrieved May 26, 2004, from http://www.soencouragement.org/comprehensive-paper-on-staff-development.htm

Caine, R., & Caine, G. (1998). Building a bridge between neurosciences and education: Cautions and possibilities. *NASSP Bulletin, 82*(598), 1–6.

Calderon, M. (1999). School reform and alignment of standards. In *Including culturally and linguistically diverse students in standards-based reform: A report on McREL's diversity roundtable I* (pp. 23–46). Aurora, CO: Mid-continent Research for Education and Learning.

California Department of Education. (2007). *Reading/Language Arts framework for California Public Schools.* Sacramento: CDE Press.

Carey, K. (2004). The real value of teachers: Using new information about teacher effectiveness to close the achievement gap. *Thinking K–16, 8*(1), 3–39.

Cawelti, G. (2003, February). Lessons from research that changed education. *Educational Leadership, 60*(5), 18–21.

Chappuis, J. (2005, November). Helping students understand assessment. *Educational Leadership, 63*(3), 39–43.

Chappuis, S., & Stiggins, R. J. (2002). Classroom assessment for learning. *Educational Leadership, 60*(1), 24–29.

Cohen, D., & Lowenberg-Ball, D. (1999, June). *Instruction, capacity, and improvement* [Electronic Version] [CPRE Research Report RR-43]. Retrieved July 3, 2004, from www.sii.soe.umich.edu/documents/instruction%20capacity%20improvement.pdf

Council of the Great City Schools. (2002). *Foundations for success: Case studies of how urban school systems improve student achievement.* Washington, DC: U.S. Government Printing Office. Retrieved November 6, 2002, from http://www.cgcs.org/reports/Foundations.html

Danielson, C. (2002). *Enhancing student achievement.* Alexandria, VA: Association for Supervision and Curriculum Development.

Darling-Hammond, L., Hightower, A., Husbands, J., LaFlors, J., & Young, V. (2002, April). *Building instructional quality: Inside-out, bottom-up, and top-down perspectives on San Diego's school reform* [Electronic Version]. Paper presented at the annual meeting of the American Educational Research Association, New Orleans. Retrieved January 11, 2004, from http://depts.washington.edu/ctpmail/PDFs/InProgress/SDCS-Reform-AERAdraft.pdf

DuFour, R., & Eaker, R. (1998). *Professional learning communities at work.* Bloomington, IN: National Educational Service.

DuFour, R., Eaker, R., & Karhanek, G. (2004). *Whatever it takes.* Bloomington, IN: National Educational Service.

Elmore, R. E. (1993). The role of local school districts in instructional improvement. In S. H. Fuhrman (Ed.), *Designing coherent education policy* (pp. 96–124). San Francisco, CA: Jossey-Bass.

Elmore, R. (2002). *Bridging the gap between standards and achievement: The imperative for professional development in education* [Electronic Version]. Washington, DC: Albert Shanker Institute. Retrieved November 1, 2003, from http://www.shankerinstitute.org/Downloads/Bridging Gap.pdf

Elmore, R., & Burney, D. (1997). *School variation and systemic instructional improvement in community school district #2, New York City.* Washington, DC: U.S. Department of Education, Office of Educational Research and Improvement, Educational Resources Information Center. (ERIC Document Reproduction Service No. 429 264)

Fuhrman, S. (1994). Challenges in systemic education reform. *CPRE Policy Briefs, 14.* Retrieved November 1, 2003, from http://www.cpre.org/Publications/rb14.pdf

Fullan, M. G. (1996, February). Future education reform. *Phi Delta Kappan, 77*(6), 420–423.

Fullan, M. (1998, April). Leadership for the 21st century: Breaking the bonds of dependency [Electronic Version]. *Educational Leadership, 55*(7). Retrieved April 13, 2004, from http://www.ascd.org/readngroom/edlead/9804/fullan/html

Garcia, E. (1999). Reforming education and its cultures. *The American Behavioral Scientist, 42*(6), 10072–11091.

Garmston, R., & Wellman, B. (1999). *The adaptive school: A sourcebook for developing collaborative groups.* Norwood, MA: Christopher-Gordon Publishers.

Garmston, R., & Wellman, B. (2000). *The adaptive school: Developing and facilitating collaborative groups* (4th ed.). El Dorado Hills, CA: Four Hats Seminars.

Gilbert, S., Hightower, A., Husbands, J., Marsh, J., McLaughlin, M., Talbert, J., & Young, V. (2002, April). *Districts as change agents: Levers for system-wide instructional improvement* [Electronic Version]. Presentation at the annual meeting of the American Educational Research Association, New Orleans. Retrieved April 13, 2004, from http://depts.washington.edu/ctpmail/PDFs/InProgress/AERA-DistrictsAsChange.pdf

Gilman, D. A., & Gilman, R. A. (2003). Standards-based teaching: Overcoming the side effects. *Principal, 83*(2), 44–48.

Glennan, T. K. Jr., & Resnick, L. (2004). School districts as learning organizations: A strategy for scaling education reform. In T. K. Glennan, Jr., S. J. Bodilly, J. Galegher, & K. Kerr (Eds.), *Expanding the reach of education reforms: Collected essays by leaders in the scale-up of educational interventions.* Santa Monica, CA: RAND.

Goodwin, B. (2000, May). Raising the achievement of low-performing students [MCREL Policy Brief]. Retrieved September 17, 2003, from http://www.mcrel.org/PDF/PolicyBriefs/5993PIPBRaisingAchievement.pdf

Guskey, T. (2005, November). Mapping the road to proficiency. *Educational Leadership, 63*(3), 32–38.

Haycock, K. (2001). Closing the achievement gap. *Educational Leadership, 58*(6), 6–11.

Hurst, D., Tan, A., Meek, A., & Sellers, J. (2003, July). *Overview and inventory of state education reforms: 1990 to 2000.* Washington, DC: National Center for Education Statistics. Retrieved November 1, 2003, from http://nces.ed.gov/pubsearch/pubsinfo.asp pubid=2003020

Jacobs, H. (Ed.). (2004). *Getting results with curriculum mapping.* Alexandria, VA: Association for Supervision and Curriculum Development.

Kohn, A. (2000). *The case against standardized testing.* Portsmouth, NH: Heinemann.

Leahy, S., Lyon, C., Thompson, M., & William, D. (2005, November). Classroom assessment: Minute by minute, day by day. *Educational Leadership, 63*(3), 18–24.

Lezotte, L., & McKee, K. (2002). *Assembly required.* Okemos, MI: Effective Schools Products.

Lindquist, M. M. (2001, October). NEAP, TIMSS, and PSSM: Entangled influences. *School Science and Mathematics, 101*(6), 286–291.

Marsh, J. (2000, September). Connecting districts to the policy dialogue: A review of literature on the relationship of districts with states, schools, and communities [Electronic Version] [CTP Working Paper #W-00-1]. Retrieved April 13, 2004, from http://depts.washington.edu/ctpmail/PDFs/District Lit.pdf

Marzano, R. J. (2003). *What works in schools.* Alexandria, VA: Association for Supervision and Curriculum Development.

Marzano, R. J., Nordford, J. S., Paynter, D. E., Pickering, D. J., & Gaddy, B. B. (2001). *A handbook for classroom instruction that works.* Alexandria, VA: Association for Supervision and Curriculum Development.

Marzano, R. J., Pickering, D. J., & Pollock, J. (2001). *Classroom instruction that works: Research-based strategies for increasing student achievement.* Alexandria, VA: Association for Supervision and Curriculum Development.

Massell, D. (2000, September). The district role in building capacity: Four strategies. *Consortium for Policy Research in Education: Policy Briefs, RB-32.* Philadelphia: Consortium for Policy Research in Education.

McLaughlin, M. W., Talbert, J. E., Gilbert, S., Hightower, A. M., Husbands, J. L., Marsh, J. A., et al. (2002, April). *Districts as change agents: Levers for system-wide instructional improvement.* Paper presented at the annual meeting of the American Educational Research Association, New Orleans.

McLaughlin, M., & Talbert, J. (2003, September). *Reforming districts: How districts support school reform.* Center for the Study of Teaching and Policy Research Report. Retrieved November 1, 2003, from http://depts.washington.edu/cepmail/PDFs/ReformingDistricts-09-2003.pdf

McTighe, J., & O'Connor, K. (2005, November). Seven practices for effective instruction. *Educational Leadership, 63*(3), 10–17.

McTighe, J., & Wiggins, G. (1999). *The understanding by design handbook.* Alexandria, VA: Association for Supervision and Curriculum Development.

Mezirow, J. (1991). *Transformative dimensions of adult learning.* San Francisco, CA: Jossey-Bass.

National Center for Educational Statistics. (n.d.). *Trends in International Mathematics and Science Study.* Retrieved July 9, 2004, from http://nces.ed.gov/timss/results.asp

Reeves, D. (2002). *Making standards work* (3rd ed.). Denver, CO: Advanced Learning Press.

Reeves, D. (2004). *Accountability for learning.* Alexandria, VA: Association for Supervision and Curriculum Development.

Reeves, D. (2006). *The learning leader.* Alexandria, VA: Association for Supervision and Curriculum Development.

Resnick, L. B. (2001). The mismeasure of learning. *Education Next, 1*(3), 78–83. Retrieved August 16, 2004, from http://www.educationnext.org.20013/78.html

Resnick, L. B., & Hall, M. W. (1998, Fall). Learning organizations for sustainable education reform. *Daedalus, Journal of the American Academy of Arts and Sciences, 127*(4), 89–188.

Resnick, L. B., & Hall, M. W. (2000). Principles of learning for effort-based education. *Education Next.* Retrieved August 16, 2004, from http://curriculum.dpsk12.org/pol_prin_learn.htm

Robitaille, D. F., Schmidt, W. H., Raizen, S., McKnight, C., Britton, E., & Nicol, C. (1993). *Curriculum frameworks for mathematics and science: TIMSS monograph No. 1.* Vancouver, Canada: Pacific Educational Press.

Sanders, W. L., & Rivers, J. C. (1996). *Cumulative and residual effects of teachers on future student academic achievement, University of Tennessee.* Knoxville, TN: Value-Added Research and Assessment Center.

Schlechty, P. (2002). *Working on the work.* San Francisco, CA: Jossey-Bass.

Schmoker, M. (2003). Tipping point: From feckless reform to substantive instructional improvement [Electronic Version]. *Phi Delta Kappan, 85*(6), 424–432. Retrieved July 3, 2004, from www.pdkintl.org/kappan/k0402sch.htm

Shepard, L. (2005, November). Linking formative assessment to scaffolding. *Educational Leadership, 63*(3), 66–70.

Sizer, T. R. (1992, November). School reform: What's missing. *World Monitor, 5*(11), 20–28.

Skaife, R., & Halstead, M. (2002). *Effective schools: Only YOU make it happen.* Phoenix, AZ: All Star Publishing.

Stiggins, R. J. (2001). *Student-involved classroom assessment* (3rd ed.). Upper Saddle River, NJ: Merrill-Prentice Hall.

Tomlinson, C. A. (2001). *How to differentiate instruction in mixed-ability classroom* (2nd ed.). Alexandria, VA: Association for Supervision and Curriculum Development.

Tucker, M. S., & Codding, J. B. (1998). *Standards for our schools: How to set them, measure them, and reach them.* San Francisco, CA: Jossey-Bass.

Tucker, P. D., & Strong, J. H. (2005). *Linking teacher evaluation and student learning.* Alexandria, VA: Association for Supervision and Curriculum Development.

U.S. Department of Education. (1997, September 23). What really matters in American education. In *Fundamental improvements are needed in public schools.* White paper prepared for the U.S. Secretary of Education speech at the National Press Club. Retrieved May 25, 2004, from http://www.ed.gov/Speeches/09-1997/part3.html

Valverde, G. A., & Schmidt, W. H. (2000). Greater expectations: Learning from other nations in the quest for "world-class standards" in US school mathematics and science. *Journal of Curriculum Studies, 32*(5), 651–687.

Wiburg, K. M. (1995). An historical perspective on instructional design: Is it time to exchange Skinner's teaching machine for Dewey's toolbox. In *Proceedings, The First International Conference on Computer Support for Collaborative Learning* (pp. 385–391). Mahwah, NJ: Lawrence Erlbaum Associates. Retrieved July 5, 2004, from http://portal.acm.org/citation.cfm?id=222863&jmp=cit&coll=portal&dl=acm

Wiggins, G., & McTighe, J. (1998). *Understanding by design.* Alexandria, VA: Association for Supervision and Curriculum Development.

Wiggins, G., & McTighe, J. (2005). *Understanding by design* (2nd ed.). Alexandria, VA: Association for Supervision and Curriculum Development.

Wisconsin Education Association Council. (n.d.). Setting the record straight: Confronting the myth of public school failure. In *WEAC Research Paper.* Madison: Author. Retrieved May 25, 2004, from http://www.weac.org/resource/may96/myths.htm

Wright, S. P., Horn, S. P., & Sanders, W. L. (1997). Teacher & classroom context effects on student achievement: Implications for teacher evaluation. *Journal of Personnel Evaluation in Education, 11*, 57–67.

Yin, R. (2003). *Case study research: Design and methods* (3rd ed.). Thousand Oaks, CA: Sage.

Index

About the Authors

Michael Moody and Jason Stricker are the founders of Insight Education Group, Inc., a consulting firm that supports teachers, schools, and districts in the implementation of high-quality standards-based instruction, instructional leadership, and academic program evaluation. They have presented at several national conferences, including the Association for Supervision and Curriculum Development, National Staff Development Council, and Phi Delta Kappa International. They have presented on a range of education topics including standards-based instruction, assessment, and leadership.

Michael S. Moody has dedicated his career to the redevelopment of educational programs in underperforming schools, which has resulted in improved school infrastructure and increased student achievement. His diverse background within the field of education, including classroom teaching, special education case management, and school leadership, enables him to provide his clients with the firsthand experience necessary to understand the needs and demands of students, teachers, and administrators. Michael holds a Doctorate in Urban School Leadership from the University of Southern California, and a Masters from the Harvard Graduate School of Education.

Jason M. Stricker has worked as a K–12 teacher, literacy consultant, and education trainer and coach. His experience in teacher education and staff development has resulted in increased student achievement and a school culture that embraces collaboration and professional development. His experience and training have allowed him to bring to projects and clients a unique and powerful perspective of how educational change affects all stakeholders at different levels. Jason holds a M.Ed. in Curriculum and Instruction from Belmont University.